The Shipwreck and the Connemara Pony

The Shipwreck and the Connemara Pony

Elaine Heney

Copyright 2022 by Elaine Heney. All rights reserved. No part of this publication may be reproduced, stored or transmitted in any form or by any means, electronic, mechanical, photocopying, recording, scanning, or otherwise without written permission from the publisher. It is illegal to copy this book, post it to a website, or distribute it by any other means without permission. This novel is entirely a work of fiction. The names, characters and incidents portrayed in it are the work of the author's imagination. Any resemblance to actual persons, living or dead, events or localities is entirely coincidental. First Edition Feb 2022 | Published by Grey Pony Films

www.greyponyfilms.com

Other books by Elaine Heney

The Connemara Adventure Series

The Forgotten Horse

The Show Horse

The Mayfield Horse

The Stolen Horse

The Adventure Horse

The Lost Horse

Saddlestone Connemara Pony Listening School

Sinead and Strawberry

Roisin and Rhubarb

Conor and Coconut

Fiona and Foxtrot

Saddlestone Pony Quiz Book

The Coral Cove Series

The Riding School Connemara Pony

The Storm and the Connemara Pony

The Surprise Puppy and the Connemara Pony
The Castle Charity Ride and the Connemara Pony

Horse Books for Kids
P is for Pony – ABC Alphabet Book for Kids
Listenology for Kids age 7-14
Horse Care, Riding and Training for kids 6-11
Horse Puzzles, Games & Brain Teasers for kids 7-14

Horse Books for Adults
Equine Listenology Guide
Dressage Training for Beginners
The Listenology Guide to Bitless Bridles
151 Polework Exercises for Horse
The Galway Connemara

"Listening to the horse is the most important thing we can do" Elaine Heney

About Elaine Heney

Elaine Heney is an Irish horsewoman, film producer at Grey Pony Films, #1 best-selling author, and director of the award-winning 'Listening to the Horse™' documentary. She has helped over 120,000+ horse owners in 113 countries to create great relationships with their horses. Elaine's mission is to make the world a better place for the horse. She lives in Ireland with her horses Ozzie & Matilda. Find Elaine's books at www.elaineheneybooks.com

Chapter 1

Branden pulled on his coat quicker than Ciara ever had seen him do so before. She giggled as he rushed around the farmhouse kitchen grabbing his gloves and little grey beanie hat. It had been almost two weeks since they had first noticed that a shipwreck had been washed up on the rocks at the side of Coral Cove. Ciara's friend Olivia had been visiting with her horse, and Ciara, Molly, and their horses, Misty and Ranger had all ridden down to the cove together. It had been Olivia that spotted the smashed ship though. Its wooden remnants hung up on the jagged black rocks that jutted out into the sea at the far end of the cove.

When they'd ridden back and excitedly told Grandad, he'd called up the authorities who'd sent out a very official-looking man and a police officer. Once they were sure the wreck was historic and no one was in any danger, they'd passed the wreck's existence onto a local maritime archaeology group and left it at that.

It was October and the weather was growing more and more gloomy. It rained more and was decidedly cooler than it had been. The man from the authorities hadn't been sure the wreck would stay wedged where it was for very long.

"Storm blew it up," he had said. "Might well blow it back again. You might find some interesting things washed ashore though in the meantime. I dare say the archaeology group will get in quick. Their season's almost over, but I doubt that'll survive the winter perched there."

The mention of 'interesting things washed ashore' had piqued Branden's interest. His friend Lucas from school had a metal detector. They'd taken it out on the farm a few times in the summer and found a lot of horseshoes, some old, some not so old. Grandad had been really pleased when they found one of Louie's that had only come off a few days before.

Ciara had enjoyed having a go with the detector too. She'd found an old toy car that Grandad remembered Mum having as a little girl. Mum had been pleased to see it and cleaned it up before putting it on a shelf on the big Welsh dresser in the kitchen.

Now though, with the prospect of washed-up shipwreck stuff, the idea of metal detecting had become much more exciting. Lucas had promised to come over on the first dry weekend day they had, so they could go and check it out. Saturday had dawned bright and sunny. Branden had been out of bed almost at the same time as Ciara.

Mum had muttered something about 'see, you can get up before 10', but just smiled.

"You about ready?" Branden asked, breaking Ciara's thoughts. Ciara nodded. Branden and Lucas had promised to watch Maddy, Ciara, and Kit the dog, while Mum and Grandad ran some errands. Since Branden wanted to check out the beach with the detector, Kit needed a walk and Ciara wanted to ride, they decided to all go down to the cove together and play on the sands for an hour or so.

"I've made some sandwiches," Mum said, getting her own coat. "And there are crisps in the pantry, fruit in the bowl, and a cake in the tin."

"Thanks Mum," Branden said. "Maddy, come on!"

Ciara's little sister appeared still looking a little sleepy around the edges. Kit, the German Shepherd following behind her, his tail wagging. Ciara smiled as he came over for a pat, though his eyes never left her sister.

"I'll go and get Misty," Ciara said as Maddy began pulling on her coat and boots. "See you later Mum."

"Bye sweetie, have a nice ride," Mum called as Ciara jogged down the hall to the front door.

Grandad was just turning Aramis and Louie, his two large grey horses, out into the paddock, as Ciara skipped across the yard. He waved at her and she waved back. Spotting her coming, Misty, her bay Connemara pony, popped her head over the door and whinnied.

"Sorry," Ciara said, rubbing her soft muzzle. "You can go play later, we're going to the cove first."

Misty's neat little ears flicked a bit and she made a whickering noise. Misty loved the beach. Ciara fetched her grooming things and dusted off any bedding and hay that had somehow accumulated on Misty overnight, before getting her tacked up and ready to go. She was just putting her saddle on when Lucas turned up on his bicycle, the metal detector strapped to his back in a strange little bag Ciara was pretty sure he'd made himself. He waved at her as he stopped the bike, its red paintwork glinting in the morning sun.

"Morning," he smiled.

"Morning," Grandad replied, wandering back from the paddock. "By, that's shiny, you been getting a new bike, Lucas?"

Lucas shook his head. "No, I just painted it. Didn't do a bad job really." He smiled, pulling his helmet off and ruffling up his longer blond hair.

"I'd say you did a very good job," Grandad said. Lucas smiled proudly. His Dad owned the local hardware store and Lucas was always pottering and tinkering with things. He'd even done some odd jobs around about last summer to get some money for a new guitar. That was Lucas's other passion, and one he shared with Branden, music. Ciara guessed that once the metal detecting was done and sandwiches were eaten, they'd probably hide out in Grandad's old garage jamming for a bit.

"Right," Grandad said, hanging up Louie's headcollar. "I'm off over to see how Davie's getting on."

Grandad's friend Davie, who owned the farm one over, had been struggling since they had moved in with Grandad while her Dad worked abroad. She'd only met him a couple of times. He was jolly and smiling, but always walked badly and used a cane.

Grandad said he'd had a stroke a few years back and it had affected his legs more than anything. But lately, he seemed to be struggling even more and Grandad was worried about him, Ciara could tell. Mac was too. Grandad, Davie, and Mac had been friends for as long as they could remember, all of them drove horses and had done shows and historic demos together. Mac had been over a few times recently and Ciara had heard them talking about how worried they were about Davie. Mac kept saying he didn't want his friend to move, but that he ought to go and live with his daughter. Grandad had agreed. They were now taking turns to nip over to Davies every other day to check on him.

"See you later," Ciara said. "Say hi to Davie for us."

"Will do," Grandad smiled and waved as he headed over to his car.

Mum left for the shops just as Ciara was mounting up, she waved as she drove past and Ciara waved back. Maddy and Branden came out and locked the door and the little group began to wander down the lane toward the cove together.

Even though it was October and the leaves were starting to turn from green to russet hues, the sun was still warm by mid-morning. It was a perfect day, Ciara mused, not too hot to ride and not too cold. Misty evidently agreed, she wandered along happily beside Branden enjoying the feel of the sunshine on her rich, rapidly thickening, bay coat.

"She's getting woolly," Branden said, reaching over and patting Misty as they walked. Misty nudged him in the arm and he made a slight oof sound.

Ciara giggled. "Maybe not the right thing to say," she said.

"Evidently," he chuckled and rubbed his arm.

Kit, who was merrily running a little way ahead and then bounding back to Maddy, his tail wagging and tongue hanging out, dived into one of the bushes sniffing about.

"Get him out of there," Branden said with a sigh. "If he rolls in something stinky Mum's going to blame me."

Maddy giggled. "Kit," she called and the dog came running, his paws going everywhere. Grandad was right, he was going to be big. He wasn't small now and he was still all paws and pointy ears. Maddy clipped on his lead and he happily fell into step beside her.

"He's coming on with his training," Lucas said, smiling at Maddy.

"Yeah, at least he doesn't hit you in the arm," Branden said.

Ciara giggled again and Misty eyed him a little. She snorted and Branden took a step closer to Lucas. They reached the road, crossed over, and wound through the dunes towards the beach.

"Do you want to go see if Molly's riding?" Branden asked as they reached the branch in the trail that ran up to Ciara's friend's cottage.

Ciara shook her head. "She had to go to town today with her Mum," Ciara said. Branden nodded.

"There are two cottages up there right?" Lucas asked.

Ciara nodded. "Molly lives in Holly Tree Cottage."

"What about the other one?" Lucas asked.

Ciara paused. She knew there was

another cottage, Yew Tree, but she'd never seen it. As far as she knew Davie owned them, he rented Holly Tree to Molly, but Yew Tree wasn't let.

"It's a bit of a wreck I think," Branden said. "At least that's what Grandad said. Davie was going to do them up and Grandad was going to help, but it never got sorted. I think it's just up from Molly's."

"I haven't seen it," Ciara said, wondering how she'd missed a whole cottage.

"It's a bit hidden I think," Branden said. "Grandad said it sits a bit lower on the bluff than Holly Tree and it's covered in ivy and behind a couple of trees."

Ciara thought hard, yes, there was a clump of trees. It was at the far side of Ranger's paddock. Ciara remembered now, it looked like an old barn or something that was overgrown. She wondered what it looked like inside, or if Molly had ever explored it, she'd have to ask her when she saw her at school on Monday.

The dunes opened out onto the sandy cove and then stopped for a second looking out over the soft sand to the sea. On calm days like today, the waves gently lapped on the shore, sprouting little white foamy peaks as they went, but on stormy days it was wild and crashing. Ciara wasn't sure which she liked more.

"Ok, here are the rules. Everyone stays on the beach, no going in the dunes or on the rocks," Branden said. "We stay within sight of each other. Kit can walk on the lead for a walk and then on the rope for a run." He pulled out one of Grandad's longlines and a giant metal thing that looked like a corkscrew it could clip onto.

"I'll walk first," Maddy said. "Then maybe I can have a go with the detector too?" she looked appealingly at Lucas.

He smiled. "Ok, but Kit has to dig for us."

Maddy smiled. "Deal," she said, shaking Lucas's hand. Kit looked from one to the other and then held a paw out to Lucas. Everyone chucked when Lucas, with a slight look of surprise on his face, took it and shook it too.

Ciara headed off on Misty alone. She liked the times they went off for a ride just the two of them. It was quiet and peaceful and free. She loved riding with Molly and Ranger, chatting to her friend as the horses happily wandered along together or cantered in the surf, but there was something about the times when it was just them alone that felt special.

Misty started to trot a little when they came to the firmer sand, keen to have their usual canter. Ciara smiled and sat in the saddle, it was all she ever really needed to do to let Misty know they could speed up. They cantered together along the cove, Misty's hooves splashing in the odd wave that lapped a little higher on the shore. Her black mane was pulled back by their speed and Ciara smiled as she felt each hoofbeat.

At the far side of the stretch of sand, they pulled up and turned back. This was the best place to see the shipwreck from. The first place they ever saw it. The hull looked as if it were merely resting on the black rocks, but Ciara knew it was snagged on them. The prow sticking up a little higher than the rest. The wood was darkened with age and missing in places, still, it was easy to see it was a ship. She wondered what it would have looked like before it sank. Was it big, with sails like something out of a film? She thought it would have been, in her mind that's how she saw it.

She and Misty headed around the sandy part of the beach, keeping a close watch on what Branden, Lucas, and Maddy were doing. Several times she heard beeping and saw one of them get excited, only to look crestfallen a few minutes later. She smiled and focused on doing a few circles on the sand in walk and trot, going one way and then the other.

Eventually though, they had enough

and headed back across the cove toward Branden and the others. They looked as if they had found something more interesting this time the beeping had gone off and Ciara was keen to see what it was.

As she rode closer, Ciara saw that the boys had laid out an old beach towel on the ground which they had put their 'finds' on. There were two tin cans, another horseshoe, a few rusty bits she couldn't identify, a couple of coins that looked like 2p's, and a nail. They'd moved down the beach to where the sand was firmer and Ciara could tell whatever they had just found was much more interesting than what was on the towel. She turned Misty and headed over to them.

Branden was smiling broadly when she came closer. He held something out as she stopped Misty beside him. Ciara looked at it with a frown. The metal object in Branden's hand looked like a fork, but not one she'd expect to find in the kitchen. Somehow it looked older and more unusual. The prongs, of which there were three, were long and thin, like a mini pitchfork, she thought. The handle too was slender and ended in a little bobble.

"Cool huh?" Branden said.

"You should keep hold of it, ask the archaeology people about it," Lucas said.

"You sure?" Branden asked.

Lucas nodded "Just let me come by if they say we can detect some more."

Branden smiled. "Of course."

"We should head back," Ciara said. "What are you going to do with your other finds?" she glanced at the towel.

"We'll take them back too," Branden said.

Lucas nodded. "Yeah, better than littering the beach."

Ciara smiled, that was true. Branden wrapped the fork in some tissue and put it in his pocket, while Maddy helped Lucas roll the other things into the towel which he stuffed into a carrier bag before they set off for home.

Chapter 2

The morning after they had been detecting on the beach, Ciara woke up early. The sun was shining and though there was a slight breeze, it still felt warm. Bouncing out of bed she hurried downstairs to find Grandad already sat at the kitchen table. He had a pile of papers and legal looking documents spread out, studying them with his glasses perched on the end of his nose. He scooped them up as she came in and headed to the fridge to get the orange juice.

"You're up early," he said with a

smile pushing the papers into a cardboard folder.

"I thought I might take Misty out while it's nice," Ciara said. "The news report last night said we might get wind and rain later."

Grandad nodded. "I heard that. I think I best get on with fixing up the sheep's winter pen. I'll put us some toast on eh?"

"Thanks," Ciara smiled.

Grandad bustled about putting toast in the toaster and putting the kettle on, while Ciara took the butter out of the fridge and found a knife.

"How's Davie?" she asked as she sat down by the table. Grandad had come home late the evening before and hadn't even seen their finds yet.

Grandad sighed. "He's alright, I suppose. I think even he knows he'd be better off going to live with Megan though. She's been asking him. I don't know what's stopping him really."

Ciara smiled a little to herself. Grandad couldn't see it, but he was just the same, never liked leaving the farm, even to come visit them. Ciara knew it was mostly the animals he worried about leaving. A day was ok, but more than that and he worried about finding someone to feed them and muck out.

"Does Megan live far away?" Ciara asked. She'd not heard much about Davies' daughter, other than her name and that she was married.

"Not so far," Grandad mused. "Closer than you and your Mum's old house. We could still drive to see him, besides, if he lived with Megan she'd be doing the cooking and keeping the place clean. He'd have time to just be himself, come out for days with me and Mac."

"Maybe he'll change his mind," Ciara said, eating her toast.

"I hope he does," Grandad said, he glanced around the kitchen. "Ain't any of us getting any younger."

A short while later, Ciara and Misty headed out across the fields behind the house. There were a few small paddocks and a large field that made up Grandad's farm, but also one of Davies that she often rode through too. As she passed through the gate into it she looked out across the fields to the dot of a farmhouse in the distance. Davies' farm wasn't all that far away, she thought, maybe she and Grandad could ride up one day so Davie could see the horses. She bet he'd like that.

They were just wandering along the field towards the bluff, Ciara still daydreaming about riding up to Davies farm, when Misty stopped. Ciara looked between her pricked little bay ears and caught sight of an old, orange camper van making its way up the drive towards Grandad's house followed by a flatbed truck with a hardtop on the back.

"I wonder who they are?" Ciara said.

Misty snorted a little in agreement, she was never bothered by traffic, so Ciara assumed her interest in the camper and truck was more of where they were and not what.

"Let's get back and find out," she said, urging Misty forward.

Apparently Misty was as keen to find out who the visitors were as Ciara and they cantered across the field towards home, pausing only to open and close the big gate. They trotted over one of the little paddocks and had just about reached the gate when

Ciara spotted Grandad chatting to a woman in a blue wool coat who had climbed out of the camper van. Ciara wondered if they were lost tourists. Plenty of people visited the area in the summer months to see the castle and beach, but there were a few who came in the autumn too. Lucas said the autumn guests were mostly surfers and people coming for days out at the castle and local museum. Grandad waved at Ciara as she opened the gate and she and Misty stepped out into the yard.

"There she is," Grandad called, waving her over. Ciara rode over beside him and Misty, seeing that his hands were in his pockets, snuffled around to see if he had anything for her. "Get out of it, my hands are cold, I've no sweets." Misty snorted a little huffily. "Ciara, this is Ruth and Ian, they're two of the team coming out to look at the wreck," Grandad said.

Ciara smiled. "Hi," she said.

"Hi," Ruth grinned, waving one hand at her. She was tall and slender with auburn hair that poked out from under her woolly hat, a smattering of freckles dashed across her nose and made her look younger than Ciara thought she probably was.

"We hear you spotted her first." Ciara looked over at the man who had climbed out of the flatbed. He was taller than Ruth with black hair and a close-cropped beard, he smiled at Ciara and fussed Misty saying hello. It made Ciara instantly like him, she nodded.

"Sort of," she said. "It was my friend who spotted it first."

"Well, we'd love to get a look at her and hear all about it," Ruth said.

"How about a cup of tea," Grandad said. "I can make one while Ciara untacks."

"Sounds great," Ian smiled.

"You should wake up Branden," Ciara said as Grandad made a move towards the house. "He's my brother," Ciara explained. "His friend Lucas has a metal detector and we all took it down to the beach yesterday for fun. He found some odd-looking fork."

"Well we'd be happy to look at it," Ruth smiled. "See if we can date it for him."

"I'll give him a shout," Grandad said.

By the time Ciara had untacked Misty and put her in the paddock with Louie and Aramis, Grandad had settled Ruth and Ian around the kitchen table with a cup of tea and a slice of cake. Maddy was up, sat in her pyjamas with Kit, mostly, on her knee staring at the strangers. Kit was still wary of new people, though Ciara wasn't sure if he sat on Maddy because he was protecting her, or if it was because she was his security blanket. Either way, Grandad took every opportunity to help educate the dog about new people and now was no exception. He encouraged the puppy off Maddy and to say hello to Ruth and Ian. Kit did so, a little half heartedly and then scampered back to Maddy's lap, his tail wagging.

Branden emerged from the living room fully dressed which surprised Ciara, it usually took him ages to get up and get ready on a weekend morning. He clutched the fork in his hand. Slipping past Ciara he placed it on the table in front of Ruth and Ian. They exchanged looks as Ciara came further into the room. Ruth picked up the fork and looked at it closely.

"Well, it's definitely a fork," she said with a smile, handing it to Ian. "And it's old."

"Spanish?" Ian speculated. "Maybe."

Ruth nodded. "I've seen similar from Spanish wrecks."

"Do you think it's from the ship?" Maddy asked, wiggling her legs. Kit licked at her and she scratched his ears and giggled.

"It's possible," Ian said. "There are lots of local stories around here, it's pretty complicated. We have one tale that says there was a Spanish shipwreck somewhere close by."

"That's right," Grandad nodded. "They say a few horses came ashore."

"Really?" Ciara asked. Grandad nodded.

"There are also stories of smugglers, people bringing in cargo to coves along the coast and hiding it in caves before selling it on the black market," Ian added.

"There's even a story that some Spanish gold from the earlier wreck washed up and was picked up by the smugglers and hidden," Ruth said. She looked at the fork. "So, what we have here is a find with no context. It could be related to the wreck. It could have washed up from another wreck somewhere else along the coast, or, if we believe the legends, it could have been from one wreck, found by smugglers and ended up in another wreck!"

"That's complicated," Maddy said with a frown.

Ruth and Ian laughed. "It is," Ruth said. "It's our job to try and un-complicate it, if we can."

"How big's your team?" Grandad asked, pouring another cup of tea.

"There are six of us usually, but Gail, our on shore finds lady is on holiday. It's pretty much the end of the season. We're not even sure if we'll get the chance to investigate the ship really, "Ruth said.

"That's why only two of us came," Ian said. "Thought we'd snag a look from the beach, see what she looks like and how interesting she might be, if we think it's safe, that sort of thing."

"And sort a campsite," Ruth added. "We don't exactly have a massive budget."

Mum came into the room and stopped looking at Maddy. "Are you not dressed yet young lady?"

Maddy giggled and slid off the chair, padding towards the door in her pink bunny slippers, Kit following her.

"Go on," Mum said, ruffling her hair. "Or you'll be late."

"Late?" Grandad asked.

"She and Kit have a playdate with Evie and her dog Pepper. Mandy and I are going to have a coffee while they play. It's at that new dog café place." Mum said.

"Looks like just us going to the beach to show Ian and Ruth the wreck then," Grandad said looking at Ciara and Branden.

"Actually," Branden looked at his shoes. "I kinda have a date." Grandad raised an eyebrow and Maddy giggled.

"Really?" Mum said. "Who with and where?"

Branden went beetroot red and Ciara felt sorry for him having to talk about it in front of the two newcomers.

"Just to the pictures," Branden said. "With Andie." Ciara smiled. Andie was the most popular girl in school and she was super nice to boot. She helped Ciara and Molly with a charity ride they'd organised a few weeks back and Ciara had thought then she and Branden got along well.

"How are you getting there?" Mum asked.

"Erm, we thought we'd get the bus from town, could you drop me on the way?" Branden asked with a smile.

"Come on," Mum said. Branden smiled. "I'm guessing you want your allowance early too."

"Please," Branden said as they wandered out into the hall.

"Just us then," Grandad said. "I'll get my coat."

Ciara had thought about riding

down to the cove, but Misty had barely looked up from the grass when they had come out of the house. As she fastened up her coat, Ciara mused that she would need to go and pick up a couple of rugs for Misty soon. Grandad said she'd need a rain sheet, something to keep her dry on wet days, and maybe a little night time rug for when it turned cold. It certainly seemed to be turning both wetter and colder to Ciara.

The morning sun was beginning to disappear behind a few straggly grey clouds and Ciara thought back to last night's weather report. Rain. With a sigh she fell into a walk beside Grandad. He glanced at the sky.

"Don't think we'll take too long down at the beach," he said.

"Nope," Ian said. "Bad weather coming in."

"Why don't you tell us how you found the wreck," Ruth said cheerfully.

Ciara smiled and nodded. She told them all about the charity ride and how Olivia, her friend from before she moved, had come over with her horse for the day. Grandad, she said, had organised for Olivia to spend the night so that the next day she could do the ride along the cove, since Ciara had told her so much about it. That was when they had spotted the wreck.

"And you saw it straight away?" Ruth asked.

Ciara shook her head. "You can see it from this end of the cove, but it's better from the far end."

They stepped out onto the sand and Ciara pointed to the little bit of the bow you could just see sticking up over the rocks. Ruth nodded.

"What are the rocks like?" Ian asked as an unusually large wave broke over them.

"Well," Grandad took a deep breath. "I tell the kids not to go near, but, truth be told, we played on them as boys. They're sharp if you fall and slippery in places, but the biggest issue is the waves. Most days, if it's calm, I'd say you'd be ok so long as you weren't alone. Days like today, well, you can see." Another large wave crested the rocks and broke over it in a roar.

"Ok," Ruth said. "Let's take a closer look, but not go on the rocks."

They walked right down to the shadow of the huge black outcrop. It was the closest Ciara had ever been to it and she brushed her fingers over the rough surface as they passed. It was hard, rough and sharp, Grandad was right, she wouldn't want to hit it. Right at the edge of the bay the rocks were low enough to see over. Ian pulled himself up just onto the rock ledge and looked at the ship.

"She's pretty precarious," he said. "But she's big, bigger than I'd expect of a smuggler's vessel."

"What are you thinking?" Ruth asked.

"Hard to see from here, but, I don't know, that might be a gun port," he strained to look. "You know I'm not sure, but she's interesting."

Ruth pulled herself up next to Ian and looked. Another wave sprayed them both and Ruth spluttered. She climbed down tugging at Ian's trouser leg as she went.

"She is interesting, but those waves are getting bigger, grab a few pictures and we'll head back and report to the team," she said.

Ian pulled out a camera phone and took a few pictures, climbing down just before a waves truck where he'd been standing. The grey clouds were gathering more now and the light seemed dimmer than it had when they set out.

"I think," Grandad said. "We should beat a hasty retreat. I don't think that's going to be just a light passing shower."

They all agreed and began to head back across the cove towards the farm. Ciara wondered if the team would get a chance to come and investigate the ship. Could it really be a Spanish vessel, the one with the horses she mused?

Chapter 3

The phone was ringing when Ciara and Grandad stepped back inside the house having seen Ruth and Ian off. Grandad picked up the receiver and smiled.

"Hey Mac," he paused. "Oh, I see, yes well it's a start and it saves us a worry over the winter. Yes, yes, I'll go over now and see if he's interested. Thanks, Mac." He put the phone down. "Best leave your coat on," he said looking at Ciara.

"Why?" Ciara asked with a smile. "Where are we going?"

"Over to the farm shop by the manor house," Grandad said, he glanced at the greying sky. "I think we can get there and back before it gets really wet."

Ciara shrugged her coat back on and followed Grandad over to his car. They climbed in and Grandad started it up, he turned the heat up a little more on the blowers.

"Bit nippy when you're out for a while isn't it," he smiled. Ciara nodded, she was wondering why they were going to the shop and if it would be rude to ask.

"Those people from the wreck investigation team seem nice," Grandad said, changing the subject.

Ciara nodded. "I don't think I'd like to stay in a tent this time of year though," she said with a shiver. "I mean, it's not like they're working in a nice dry place during the day, coming back to a tent would be awful in the rain afterwards."

Grandad frowned. "Never thought of that," he said thoughtfully.

They drove on for a while in silence, Ciara watching the scenery roll by and the even greyer clouds roll in. She was just wondering what to get Olivia for her birthday later that month when she realised they were at the farm shop already. Ciara hadn't been to the shop before, though she had met Farmer Bob that owned it, he'd brought a little van of produce over to the charity ride they had done. Grandad pulled the car in and they clambered out. The shop was wooden with a big window displaying some of the things sold inside, a little stall was set up by the door with a few crates on it full of fruit and veg. Ciara liked it instantly.

Grandad swung the door open and a little bell chimed as they stepped inside. Here there were shelves of soaps and lotions in different scents, as well as more produce. Farmer Bob, a large smiling man with dark hair and a beard came into the shop from a little back room and waved at them.

"All right Patrick, don't see you in

much, what can I do you for?" the man asked.

"Actually, Bob I'm here about sheep," Grandad said with a smile as Ciara went to look at some of the things on the shelves.

"Sheep?" Farmer Bob said.

"Well, rumour has it you were looking to put a few animals in paddocks by the shop, sort of a petting deal for the kids," Grandad said.

"Aye," Farmer Bob nodded. "It was my assistant shopkeeper Clodagh's idea, or rather her friend Rachel's. Seems that's what she wants to do when she grows up, turn her Grandparent's old place into a place kids can come and meet all sorts of farm animals. Girls thought it would be nice to do a sort of mini version here and I don't disagree." Bob frowned. "You're not giving up the sheep though, are you?"

"No," Grandad smiled. "Davie Willis is." Bob nodded as if understanding. "He's got maybe six ewes left, he doesn't want them to go to slaughter or anything, but he's struggling, me and Mac are helping out, but with winter coming on..." Bob nodded again. "Anyway, Mac was telling him the rumours and he said if Bob wants sheep for the young'uns to see he can have mine. So, here I am."

"Well," Bob said, rubbing his beard. "I'd have to give him something for them."

Grandad held a hand up. "He said no charge, it'd help him out really Bob, he just wants them safely homed somewhere."

"Still," Bob said.

"If you can collect them and tell him he can stop over and see them when he likes he'd be made up," Grandad said.

Bob smiled broadly. "Alright then," he said. "Tell him to give me a few days, I'll have to sort out a paddock and some shelter."

Grandad shook Bob's hand warmly. "I'll tell him, thanks."

"Thank you," Bob said cheerily. "Reckon I best call Clodagh to round up her troops, they can get started clearing out some of that paddock by the shop."

Ciara found a little golden horse key chain hanging on a little rack by the candles, it was perfect. She pulled it off the hook and came to stand by Grandad.

"Could I get this please," she said to Farmer Bob.

"Certainly, you take it, no charge, your Grandad's just sorted me a flock of sheep, the least I can do is pass on a keychain," he grinned.

"Are you sure?" Ciara asked. "They aren't our sheep."

Grandad chucked, but Farmer Bob leaned over the counter to her and smiled. "Well then, you think of this as a kind act and pay it forward," he said.

"Thanks," Ciara smiled. "It's going to be a gift for my best friend from our old town, it's her birthday soon."

"In that case, I hope she likes it," Bob said with a grin.

Bob waved to them as they left the shop and headed back to Grandad's car. A few little drops of rain hit the windshield as Ciara fastened her seatbelt and Grandad started the engine.

"You think Olivia will like it?" she asked.

Grandad nodded. "I'm sure she will."

"Grandad," Ciara asked, he glanced at her. "If Davie does go to live with Megan, what happens to the cottages?"

Grandad didn't say anything for a moment and Ciara felt her heart speed up a little. Molly's parents rented the cottage from Davie and if he moved, well, he could sell it.

"I don't know," Grandad said eventually. "Davie's always refused to leave the farm because he doesn't want it sold to someone who would develop it. Same reason the cottages were bought up. Nothing might change at all."

Ciara nodded her head, but she still felt a little worried. What if Davie did sell and Molly had to move?

Even if she didn't move far away, it might still mean they couldn't ride together, and someone else would move in. She stopped herself, there were too many 'ifs' to start worrying about. One thing at a time, Davie hadn't even agreed to move yet, just let the sheep go.

The rain was beginning to fall in fat drops by the time they got home, and the horses were lined up at the gate wanting to be inside before the weather really came in. Ciara darted through the rain and grabbed the headcollars while Grandad parked the car. They brought all three in at the same time. Ciara had just closed Misty's door when it really started pelting down. She shuddered a little, the damp making it feel colder than it was.

"You get the feeds," Grandad said over the roar of the rain. "I'll lock the chickens up, might as well get done and in for the night, this isn't stopping for a while."

Ciara nodded. She fetched the horse's buckets from the little shed behind their stables, remembering to close and bolt the door as she went. She slipped the three feeds into the stables, pausing to watch as Misty stuffed her nose happily into her purple bucket, steam wafting up from her rump as she began to dry off. She really would need to go to

Lowells and get that rain sheet.

Mum pulled up with Maddy, Branden, and Kit, just as Grandad was stoking the fire in the living room. Suddenly the house sprang into life, Branden was pulling off his wet coat and trying not to tell Mum how his date went, while Kit jumped about excitedly and Maddy rattled on about how much fun she had with Evie.

"Dinner's on," Grandad said.

"Oh, thanks Dad," Mum said, gathering the wet coats and taking them to the boot room to hang up.

"What are we having?" Branden asked.

"Jacket potatoes with cheese, ham, and butter," Grandad said.

"Sounds yummy," Maddy said.

Mum came in rubbing her wet hair. "It's raining cats and dogs out there."

As if to confirm this there was the sound of rain lashing against the windows. Ciara peeked around the side of the tick curtains out into the yard. It was dark now and she could barely make out the white-painted stables, the rain was bouncing off the yard and pelting the windows.

"Yuck," Ciara said.

"Let's have tea in here with the fire shall we," Grandad said.

Everyone agreed. The living room, with its comfy chairs and roaring fire, seemed much more inviting on nights like this than the kitchen. Grandad began putting out potatoes on plates and Mum poured everyone a drink, promising Coco later. Ciara smiled. It had been ages since they'd had hot cocoa.

While they ate they caught up on the events of the day. Grandad and Ciara told everyone about seeing the ship, Davie's sheep, and Farmer Bob. Maddy told everyone about playing with Evie and the dogs, who got along great and now were besties. Mum said she was happy just to talk to another Mum other than Faye and have a coffee, while Branden steadfastly refused to say anything other than it was a great movie. He blushed though and Ciara giggled.

After dinner, Ciara helped with drying the dishes and Branden with putting them away, while Mum made the coco.

"Grandad," Ciara said thoughtfully. "You know you said you knew the legend about the shipwreck? Well, could you tell us it?"

Grandad smiled as he handed her a plate. "Well, it's a good night for it. Yes, I think that's a great idea, huddled around the fire, hot cocoa," he nodded.

Soon enough Ciara found herself doing just that, huddled around with everyone else in the cosy living room, her cocoa in hand. She sniffed at the steaming mug and took a sip; it was hot and sweet and warming. The perfect antidote to the raging rains outside.

"It's still pouring," Mum said, closing the door to the kitchen and taking a seat.

Grandad nodded. "And if legend is right, it was a night just like this one the wreck went down on."

"Really?" Maddy asked her mouth wide open. Kit lay on her knee asleep, shifted a little as she spoke.

Grandad nodded. "It was 1588. Queen Elizabeth the first rules England, and she is about to be confronted by the Spanish," Grandad said with a smile. "An armada of ships set sail from Lisbon and headed to

England planning to help invade. They sailed towards the channel and were met by our own ships there. They outgunned us, but the English ships knew the waters and were faster and more manouverable. The two fleets tangled over a few days before the Armada managed to reach Calais. While they were anchored there, the British sent in fireships."

"What's a fireship?" Maddy piped up.

"It's when you set one of your ships, or one you captured or something, on fire and steer it into another group of ships," Branden said.

"Very good," Grandad smiled. "That's right, you see ships back then were wooden, so fire was an effective weapon."

Maddy's mouth made a little O shape and she nodded, the orange glow of the fire somehow making the idea of a fireship much more real. Ciara snuggled further into the sofa and listened intently.

"The fireships scattered the armada and then there was a big battle between the two fleets. Several ships sank, others fled badly damaged. Pursued by the British fleet, and with the weather not favourable, the armada had no choice but to sail up, around Britain, up around Scotland, and then past Ireland to get home. A lot of the ships didn't make it, including, if you believe it, one on our little stretch of coast." Grandad paused for effect and Ciara smiled.

"Legend has it that one night, shortly after the big battle, it was stormy and raining. A local man living close to the cove looked out and saw great white sails waving in the storm-tossed sea, for a second he saw the ship and then it was suddenly tossed towards the rocks. The man rushed for help and rounded up the fishermen from town, but the sea was so rough they weren't sure they could reach any survivors. They didn't know whose ship it was, you see. They rowed out towards the ship, calling into the night. They could hear calls back, but no one knew what was being said, it was all in Spanish you see. Then, through the night they saw them. Several large white horses seemed to spring from the sea itself. The men thought they were ghosts at first, but one brave man, well, they say he leapt in and grabbed one of the horse's manes, rode it towards the shore, guiding it, the others following. They were soaked, scared, and shivering, but alive. The men took the horses and kept them, but the ship slipped beneath the waves."

"Wow," Ciara said.

"That sounds far-fetched," Branden said.

"Well, some horses did wash

ashore in Ireland for sure," Ciara said. "I learned that in history class at school. They bred in with local horses and helped create the Connemara we have today."

"Well, there's more," Grandad said. "See a long time later there were smugglers using caves along the coast to bring in goods illegally. Goods ships would add a bit on here and there and drop it off in boats close to the cove. They say that one night, on a very low tide, one of the ships heading in to drop goods off ran over something sticking out of the sea."

"The Spanish ship," Ciara said.

Grandad nodded. "It caused so much damage that the goods ship began to take on water and sink. She managed to limp up the coast and was saved, but the men who set out to receive her illegal goods went back as soon as they could to see what she hit. A few men dived down and found a scattering of gold coins and a few trinkets. Keen to find more they hid the treasures in the cave with the illegally smuggled goods. Not long after they were arrested and in those days it was a hanging offence smuggling." Grandad said.

"Hang on," Branden put in. "If they were hung, who told the story?"

Mum giggled. "I remember this one, one man, one man escaped to tell the tale, but he never got back to the cove to retrieve his loot and it's still there, hidden to this day!" she laughed.

"Laugh if you like Laura," Grandad smiled. "I remember you digging up the garden looking for that treasure."

Mum reddened a little and Branden snorted. "I like the story," Maddy said sleepily. "I hope it's true and that the horses got to live nice lives and not have to go to any battles."

"Me too," Ciara agreed.

"Come on," Mum said. "Bedtime for you lot." Ciara stood up and helped Maddy move Kit before they headed upstairs, the sound of the rain still hitting the windows. She wondered if the story really was true

.

Chapter 4

Ciara and Molly glanced at each other as they walked along the corridor toward their classroom for registration. Most people were chatting about half-term plans and Halloween, but once or twice Ciara was sure she heard people talking about the wreck.

"News travels fast," Molly said.

"I'll say," Ciara replied. "I hope the cove doesn't end up packed with sightseers."

"I just hope people don't turn up and try to dive on it looking for treasure," Molly said, rolling her eyes. Ciara agreed. The team investigating the wreck couldn't turn up fast enough really.

They headed into their family unit for registration, sliding into their usual seats in the corner at the back. They were just settling in when their friend Orla rushed in just in time, and threw herself into a seat. She looked a little gloomy and Ciara wondered why.

"We can't have the party," she said with a sigh.

Ciara knew instantly what she was talking about, the Halloween party. Orla's Dad was the manager at the local castle which had recently been bought by a wealthy American man.

Mr. Lewellin was super nice and had spent a lot of money doing the castle up so it could re-open to the public. He had been hoping to open the castle by the week of half-term and had agreed that Orla could help organise a Halloween party for kids in the area if they were ready. Orla had been really excited about it, as had Ciara and Molly.

"What happened?" Molly asked.

"The work's not done," Orla said simply. "No way the workmen will be finished for half term. Mr. Lewellin says it's better that it's done properly than done twice. He's talking about waiting until the spring now," she looked a little sad. "I guess he's right,

I mean, no one will really come much in the winter, other than at Christmas time I suppose."

Ciara glanced at Molly feeling disappointed but not wanting to show it. "Well, it's not so bad is it," she tried to smile. "Maybe we could have our own little party or something. I could ask Grandad. Maybe we could have a sleepover and watch Halloween cartoons or something."

Orla shook her head but smiled. "I was so disappointed about the party. Dad said something similar, but then he remembered there was this residential driving course he'd seen advertised," she positively beamed. "He's agreed to book us on it."

"You can't drive though," Molly said. "You don't have a license."

Orla laughed. "Oh, no, not a car, Teddy! It's for driving horses, you stay in these amazing cabins in the woods close to this big old house, or castle, or something like that, and you get instruction on driving horses and there are loads of trail rides in the woods. Dad said we can take Paddy too!"

"Wow," Molly said smiling. "That sounds amazing. How long are you going for?"

"A week," Orla said. "We're going on Saturday and coming back the following Sunday morning. I won't see you guys all half term." Her face fell for a second as if she'd only just realised the face.

"Yeah, but you'll have an amazing time," Molly pointed out.

"And take pictures," Ciara smiled. "We want to see."

"Promise," Orla grinned again. "And Dad says you can come for the sleepover one Saturday when we're back, I could show you the photos then!"

"Great," Ciara smiled just as the bell for first-class rang out and they headed off their separate ways, Ciara and Molly to History, Orla to P.E.

"What should we do for Halloween then?" Molly asked as they wandered down the corridor together. "We should do something."

"We could still do the cartoon thing," Ciara smiled. "What do you normally do on Halloween?" she asked. This was Ciara's first Halloween at Grandad's and she wasn't exactly sure what to do.

"Not much, "Molly sighed. "I bet you used to go trick or treating."

Ciara nodded. "Yep, every year we'd come home from school, watch a Garfield Halloween, change into our costumes and we'd go Trick or Treating. Dad always brought pizza home with him and we'd watch a Scooby-doo movie marathon while we ate it. Then we could raid whatever we got from trick or treat before bed.

Branden always got to stay up a bit later to watch some cheesy horror film, but Mum never lets him watch anything really scary."

"That sounds nice," Molly said.

"It was. Mum is still trying to keep things the same, but it isn't really. She brought the Halloween decoration box out, but no one's bothered putting up things. She said we can still do the movie thing and get pizza. I think Maddy's going to miss trick or treating though."

"You could come to mine and trick or treat," Molly said.

Ciara smiled. "Thanks, but one house doesn't really seem like trick or treating."

"We could put bowls of sweets out in front of Niblet and Ranger's stables," Molly suggested.

Ciara giggled. "I think Niblet would object if they weren't for him," she said thinking about the long-eared donkey that shared a paddock with Molly's chestnut Arab.

"True," Molly agreed.

"The party would have been good, it would have been different but in an exciting way," she sighed.

"Maybe we could still have one," Molly said. "We could just have a small one, just us."

Ciara thought for a moment and smiled. "Do you think it might be warm enough for a beach party? We could light a fire and have smores."

"Ooohh," Molly said. "And tell moderately creepy stories around the campfire."

Ciara giggled. "Yeah."

"We should check out the forecast," Molly said, linking her arm with Ciara.

"You know," Ciara said thoughtfully. "Back at riding school they always had a Halloween ride. We'd dress up and ride around this little trail at the back of the riding school. It was already lit up anyway because it was the way to the field, but we all had torches and things. It was really cool."

"We could do that," Molly smiled. "We could ride to the cove and back."

Ciara thought for a second. "Maybe we should do it at sunset though, so we're just coming back in the dark. I could ask Grandad or Branden to walk with us for the road bit."

"That would be amazing," Molly said. "Imagine riding in the cove on Halloween night with lanterns or something!"

Ciara suddenly felt much more excited about the idea. "We could do it before the beach party. Maybe we could even invite a few people."

"Who?" Molly asked.

Ciara thought for a second. "Well, Maddy's made this new friend, Evie and I bet Branden's friends Luke, James, and Liam would come, they could play some music. Plus, Branden had a date."

"Who with?" Molly asked.

"Andie," Ciara said.

"No way!" Molly giggled. "For real?"

Ciara nodded. "Mum's been teasing him about it all weekend."

"We do need to check the weather," Molly said, chuckling. "Do you think Olivia could come?"

Ciara shook her head. She had hoped to see Olivia during the holidays, especially since it was her birthday. "Nope. I called to invite her over anyway, it's her birthday during the break, but her Mum asked me not to."

"How come?" Molly asked.

"Well, I guess I can tell you," she smiled. "Her Mum and Dad are surprising her with a trip to see her Nona Marie in Italy, she has no idea."

"Really?" Molly asked.

Ciara nodded. "Yep, her Nona lives in Tuscany, she hasn't seen her in ages, and she's not been out to Nona's place in like, five years or something. She's going to freak out when she finds out."

"How are they going to surprise her, do you know?" Molly asked.

"Yeah, they told her that her Dad has to go away for a few days with work and they're taking him to the airport to see him off, only when they get there they're going to tell her the truth," Ciara said.

Molly's mouth dropped open. "We're going to hear her scream from here."

Ciara laughed. "Probably," she said as they stepped through the classroom door and went to find a seat.

The school day passed slowly, but by the end of it, Ciara and Molly were determined to do 'something' for Halloween. Their top choice was definitely a beach party and ride, so the first thing Ciara did when she got home was to go and find Grandad to ask him about the possibility. He was in the kitchen with the same manilla folder she'd found him with before, sifting through things. She'd not really thought much of the paperwork and the folder before, but seeing Grandad with it twice made her wonder what it was.

"Are those bills?" she asked, pouring herself a drink.

Grandad looked up and smiled. "No, no," he sighed. "It's just some paperwork I need to sort out with Davie."

"Did you go up today?" she asked, slipping into a chair near Grandad.

"I did. I helped Farmer Bob sort out the sheep. They've all gone off down to their new home today," Grandad smiled. "Perfect for a petting paddock he said. I don't disagree but I hope he remembers their names because I can't." He chuckled.

"You remember your sheep's names," Ciara pointed out.

"True," Grandad said and smiled. "What are you up to then?"

Ciara grinned. "Molly and I were wondering if we could organise a beach party."

"A beach party," Grandad laughed. "It's autumn here, not summer in California!"

Ciara smiled. "We know that, we were thinking we could have had a little fire and made smores and told creepy stories on Halloween."

"Oh," Grandad smiled. "I see. Well, it'll be dependent on the weather that. It can turn on a dime as they say. I tell you what if I were you two I'd organise it but plan to move it somewhere inside if need be."

"Where?" Ciara asked.

"Well, there's the garage," Grandad suggested. "Unless Faye has any ideas." Ciara made a note to ask Molly if her Mum had a suggestion for them, then she paused, a thought crossing her mind.

"What about the other cottage, the empty one? If we didn't make a mess and tidied up after ourselves, do you think Davie might let us go there?" she asked.

Grandad smiled. "Maybe, but he's a bit busy at the moment."

"Busy?" Ciara asked.

Grandad nodded and stood up heading over to the stove to help himself to some more coffee from the pot.

"He's decided to move in with Megan," Grandad said. "He told me this morning. With the sheep sorted he's got no animals left except old Rusty the dog and he can go with Davie."

Ciara paused for a second. "Wait," she said, almost fearful to ask. "What, what does that mean for the farm and the cottages?"

Grandad paused with his hand on the coffee pot. "Nothing for now," he said, pouring the hot brown liquid into the mug.

"But eventually?" Ciara asked.

"I'm not sure," Grandad said sitting down. "And I don't want you running off and telling Molly anything just yet, don't get her upset. Davie's talking things over with Megan and with me and I promise as soon as he knows what he's doing I'll let you know. There's a good chance he's going to keep on renting the cottage as it is. The farm's a different matter." Ciara waited patiently for him to go on. Grandad sighed. "Davie never did want to sell it, he hates the idea someone might come along and develop the land. He's being stubborn about it, says he won't sell it, he'll rent it on some long-term lease, but I don't know if he'll find anyone to take it on like that." Grandad shook his head.

"What about Megan, doesn't she want it?" Ciara asked.

"No," Grandad said. "She's not a farmer, never has been, she's happier in a cottage surrounded by pretty places she doesn't need to take care of. Me and Mac thought about offering to split the land between us, but neither of us needs that much. I offered to take the backfield, the one you ride in and Mac said he'd take the field by his southern border, but there's still three big fields, two barns, and a paddock." Grandad shook his head. "Mac and I have been asking around, see if we could find anyone interested in it. Bit like the sheep really, if you find the right match Davie'll budge."

The image of Niblet and a carrot sprang into Ciara's head. She wished she were older and could take on the farm. She and Olivia had always said they'd buy a farm together and have ponies. Davies would be ideal for that. Grandad sighed bringing her back to reality.

"Ah, something will come up, I'm sure. In the meantime, Mac and I said we'd go up and help Davie start packing things. Sort out this stuff," he waved the paperwork in his hand. "Megan's coming at the weekend to stay with him and help out. She can't in the week, she's at work."

"We can help, if you need it," Ciara said. "Move boxes and things I mean, not paperwork."

"I'll bear that in mind," Grandad said with a grin. "But you best be focusing on this Halloween party I think and I mean it, no telling Molly. I know she's your friend and you worry and you'll think you need to tell her, but you don't, not until we know what's happening. I meant what I said, when I know you know. Honestly," Grandad said. "I doubt he'll sell up unless it's to someone he knows won't develop it. Mind, this might be the push we need to get Yew Tree sorted," he mused as he shuffled off towards the door with his coffee in one hand and the folder in the other.

Ciara sat in the kitchen for a moment thinking over what Grandad had said. Could she really not tell Molly? It seemed wrong not to, but Grandad was right, really she didn't know anything. Somehow though she still felt like she was keeping secrets and she didn't like it at all. After a second thought she jumped up and headed upstairs to the phone determined to call Olivia and ask her what she thought about the whole thing, after all, Grandad hadn't said anything about telling her what was happening.

Chapter 5

Ciara looked out of the window at the pouring rain and sighed. It was the first day of the holidays and it was a washout. The rain had been steadily falling since before dawn and showed no signs of stopping. Misty was standing in the paddock happily grazing in the new rain sheet Grandad had picked up for her from Lowells the day before. It was purple and silver. Ciara wasn't sure if it suited Misty or not, but she decided as long as it kept her dry it didn't really matter.

She had been supposed to be

riding with Molly that morning, starting the holidays as they meant to go on, but there was no chance of that today. Ciara didn't consider herself a fair-weather rider. She didn't mind getting damp in drizzle or fog, but in this, she'd have been soaked through by the time she reached the end of the drive. Ciara sighed again.

"It's not that bad," Mum said from her seat on the couch. She put down her knitting and looked over at Ciara. "I'm sure there's something you could all do." Mum glanced from Ciara to the equally sorry-looking Maddy who sat rolling a ball to Kit.

"We can't go outside and play," Maddy pointed out. "We can't even go in the playhouse, it's too cold and wet."

"Well, we just need to think of something to do indoors," Mum said with a smile. "Maybe some painting or colouring? You could make some Halloween decorations."

"Why," Maddy huffed. "No one's going to see them."

"We are," Mum said a little firmly.

"Me and Molly were thinking of doing a Halloween ride to the cove, you could come and bring Kit," Ciara said with a smile. "We could go in fancy dress, I bet there's stuff in the old fancy dress box we could put together for a costume." Maddy glanced up at her, the flicker of a smile on her face.

Mum smiled. "Grandad said you were thinking about that, and maybe a party on the beach too."

"A party, really?" Maddy said suddenly, smiling. Ciara winced. She'd decided not to tell Maddy in case the weather was bad and they couldn't hold it after all, but she guessed the cat was out of the bag now. She nodded. "We will need costumes then," Maddy said, bouncing up off the floor.

"Hold on," Mum said. "Ciara, why don't you call Molly, I bet she's as fed up as you. Ask her if she has any dress-up bits laying around. You can toss the lot on the floor and rake through them together, keep you all out of mischief."

"Thanks Mum," Ciara called as she leapt off her chair and raced to the phone.

As it turned out Molly had been as bored as Ciara and she did have an old assortment of costumes and bits stuffed in a box. Half an hour later Molly was in Ciara's living room with the box in hand ready to dump its contents onto the floor, while Mum and Faye stood in the doorway watching. Ciara and Maddy fetched their own things, and some of Branden's from years before, and they threw everything onto the rug. The floor was suddenly covered in a riot of colours, fabrics, and accessories, a little black cat headband perched precariously on the top.

"Well," Faye said. "That should keep you going."

Mum smiled. "One teenager happily making loud music in the garage, check. Three girls with a pile of costumes, check."

"Coffee?" Faye smiled.

Mum grinned and nodded. "Check," she said.

They began to rummage through the old costumes, trying on the various accessories there. Ciara put on one of Branden's old cowboy hats along with a feather boa that Maddy had once worn. Everyone laughed.

"Oh, I remember this," Molly

giggled, pulling out a pointy witch's hat with purple hair glued to it. She put it on her head, but it was too small to fit properly. She pulled it off and plopped it down on Maddy's head, Maddy giggled and put on a pair of pink, oversized novelty sunglasses.

"Witch on vacation," she laughed and flopped down on a chair.

"We should probably wear something we can ride in," Molly pointed out.

Ciara nodded. "And definitely Halloween-like."

"This could be a good ghost outfit," Molly suggested pulling out a white robe-type dress. "It's wide enough to ride in."

"That was last Christmas's nativity costume. Angel no.3," Ciara said. "But we could totally ghost it up.

"You need face paint," Maddy said, pulling something from the pile. She handed a little box of face paint to Ciara who nodded.

"Yeah, we can paint your face white maybe," she suggested.

"It's definitely a possibility," Molly said.

"Let's make a possible pile on the couch," Ciara said.

They began to sort through the things on the floor and soon had a pile of outfits that were too small for any of them, even Maddy, or that just wouldn't work for Halloween. As they were sorting through Molly pulled out a large Santa suit.

"Whose is this?" she giggled.

"That's Dad's," Ciara laughed. "He used to pretend to go in the shower and then come downstairs dressed in it and pretend to be Santa."

"Except he never fooled us, "Maddy said defiantly. "Everyone knows Santa is a jolly fat man with a real beard. Dad is not that fat and his beard was so fake."

"No reindeer either," Molly pointed out. Maddy nodded her head in agreement.

They were just adding the last few things to the pile on the couch when the phone rang and Mum padded into the hall to answer it.

"Hello, oh, hello, yes, right, I see," she said. "Well, thanks for letting me know." She hung up.

"Who was it Mum?" Ciara asked.

"The wreck team, a nice lady, called herself Jen I think, said they're not coming down until Monday now because of the weather. I hope they find somewhere to stay better than that field they were planning on camping in, it'll be a bog after this," she said looking out of the window.

Ciara glanced out at the grey drabness outside. It was still raining, she sighed. As fun, as it was sorting out costumes, looking out at the wet weather, made her doubt they'd need them. She turned away, trying to think positively.

At last, the costumes were divided up and they stuffed those that were no good back into various boxes and bags before turning their attention to the couch. Mum and Faye came in to see what they'd found.

Maddy had decided she liked the witches hat that Molly brought. Molly said she could have it, so Maddy constructed her witch's costume around it. She'd found a thick purple skirt that had once been Ciara's, a small broomstick with a few broken bristles, and a cloak that she had worn the year before made from crushed velvet.

"What about a top?" Ciara said.

"I'll wear my black jumper," she said.

"Good idea," Mum said. "It'll keep you nice and warm."

"That's a good point," Ciara said. "Whatever we wear needs to be warm enough. We don't want to have this amazing costume and cover it in our coats."

Molly looked at the tangle of costumes and then smiled. "I think I have it."

She brushed aside the old angel costume, and another witch's dress and pulled out a few bits from the pile.

"We can be pirates, it'll fit with the wreck and be easy to ride in," she pulled out two of Branden's old costume shirts. "These are huge on us. We can put a jumper under them and put our thick jods on too."

"And these," Ciara said, smiling and pulling out two old scarves. "We can use these as belts."

"You need hats and these," Maddy said, she handed Ciara and Molly two plastic swords and they giggled.

"Yeah, hats could be an issue," Molly said.

"No, not really," Mum said. She reached in and pulled out two more old silk scarves. "You could just tie these around your helmets."

Ciara smiled. "Should we try them on?"

"YES!" Maddy said loudly, snatching

her things and darting upstairs.

Maddy was ready first and went rushing down to show Mum and Faye. Ciara found herself alone with Molly and her thoughts turned to Davie and the move. She'd talked over with Olivia her dilemma and not gotten very far. Olivia could see the problem, but not really the answer. They both agreed that Grandad was right, they didn't know what would happen and it could worry Molly unnecessarily if Davie didn't sell in the end. That being said they also both agreed Molly should know what was going on because if he did sell and she found out later Ciara had known all along, her feelings could be hurt. Moreover, they both agreed if it were them, they'd want to know. The arguments for and against telling Molly had been playing on Ciara's mind and she'd gone back and forth over them. She'd even talked over the problem with Misty to no avail. Usually talking over things with the little bay mare helped her make a decision, but she was as lost as ever about it. One of the worst things though was when she thought back to just before they moved in with Grandad. She had hated that no one had told her there was a possibility that Dad would go abroad to work for at least a year, or that that could mean a move. Ciara sighed.

"Ta-da," Molly said, spinning around

in her pirate costume. Ciara smiled. Yes, it was cobbled together from bits, but it looked great. Ciara smiled. Molly turned to leave, ready to show her mum.

"Molly," Ciara said, she took a deep breath as Molly turned back toward her.

"What's up?" Molly asked.

Ciara sighed as Molly came back and sat on the bed. "If you knew something you thought a friend should know, but it might not ever happen, would you tell them anyway?"

"I don't think I understand," Molly said. Ciara thought for a second, she decided Molly needed to know the facts, not the what if's. Grandad had told her not to tell Molly what if's, but Davie moving in with Megan wasn't a what-if, it was a fact.

Ciara swallowed hard. "Davie's moving. He's going to go and live with his daughter, Megan," she said quietly. She let the fact hang in the air for a moment. From the look on Molly's face, Ciara knew she understood what implications Davie moving might bring.

"Do you, I mean, is he going to sell the cottage?" Molly asked.

Ciara shook her head. "I don't know. Grandad doesn't think so, he doesn't think Davie would sell to anyone who might develop it. You can't tell anyone I told you," she said, suddenly a little worried. "I promised

Grandad I wouldn't, but I couldn't not tell you."

Molly nodded and Ciara wrapped an arm around her shoulders. "I'm sorry," she said.

Molly smiled. "It's ok, Davie should move in with Megan, it's better for him. Besides, I've met him, I think your Grandad's right, he'll probably just keep things as they are. I mean I would if I was him. He'll get a little money every month from renting out the cottage, he can use it to do stuff," Molly mused.

Ciara smiled, she hadn't thought of that before, it was true. She contented herself thinking that Grandad and Molly were right.

Positive thinking, she told herself, everything will be fine.

"I'm glad you told me though," Molly said.

"Me too," Ciara smiled. She felt a ton lighter.

"Come on," Molly said. "We should show our Mum's."

They stood up and headed downstairs. "Do you think we should dress the horses up too?" Ciara asked as they went.

Molly shook her head. "I don't need to, besides what would we dress them up as a ship?"

Ciara laughed. "I doubt Ranger would like that."

"He'll probably shy at my scarf

hat," Molly added.

Grandad was back when they came downstairs. Ciara noticed he still had the manilla folder tucked under his arm, but he seemed happier than he had done in the last few days. He was watching Maddy twirl around the room while Kit tried to grab her broom.

"I think we might need to mend that before Halloween," he said pointing at the few pathetic bristles still clung to the end of the shank. "I reckon there's some stuff in the shed we could use."

"Thanks, Grandad," Maddy said.

"Oh, and here come the pirates of the Caribbean," he said laughing as

Ciara and Molly walked in. Ciara smiled.

"Watch out for cannon," Faye added.

"Oh, speaking of ships and cannons," Mum said. "The wreck team rang Dad, they're coming Monday, the weather's too bad for the weekend."

"I thought they might postpone," Grandad said cheerily. "Good job they have, that field they want to camp in is a washout."

"What are they going to do?" Faye asked.

"Well," Grandad said with a smile. "I've been up at Davies and we thought they might like to be your neighbours for a week or two," he said looking at

Faye.

"Yew Tree," Faye said with a smile.

Grandad nodded. "I was hoping to get a few hands to come down and check her over, clear things up a bit. I mean it's a wreck itself, but we could clean it out, sort the fire. At least it's four solid walls for them to sleep in, and I dare say warmer and drier than a tent."

"Well I'm sure that's true," Faye said with a raised eyebrow. "But still, be quite a job."

"That's ok," Mum said with a smile. "I'm sure Ciara, Maddy, and Branden can help us Dad. Besides, the team themselves could do a bit to make it comfortable. I'm sure they'd appreciate it a lot."

"Did you get a number for them?" Grandad asked. Mum nodded. "Give them a ring then eh, Laura, tell them about the cottage and that we'll go down and sort it a bit over the weekend. We can go after lunch, the rains easing a little, but I doubt it'll stop totally."

"I'll go now," Mum said. "Branden's in the garage with Luke, maybe we can persuade him to help out too."

"Can I help?" Molly asked. "I know you're going into town Mum, but I don't want to traipse around the supermarket really."

Faye smiled. "If it's ok with Laura and Pat."

"More the merrier," Grandad said. Ciara smiled at Molly. She had been keen to see Yew Tree cottage for ages, and the idea of getting to go inside and explore it with Molly was even more exciting. Suddenly the damp rainy day was looking up, even if it didn't include a ride.

Chapter 6

Grandad pulled some ivy away from the front door of the little cottage. Yew Tree was hidden from view, partly by a few large Yew trees that gave it its name, and partly by the ivy that covered its old stone walls. Ciara peered at the little cottage with a smile. It was small and neat, much more so than the larger Holly Tree. There was an odd sort of barn attached to the side that she and Molly had sheltered in while Grandad pulled away the vegetation. It looked as though it had once been stalls for animals, but now it was empty, the wooden partitions rotting in place.

"We should sweep this out," Molly said. "It'd be a great place to store stuff for them." Ciara agreed. They left Grandad, Branden, and Luke wrestling with the greenery and jogged up the short path that led through an overgrown tangle of plants and weeds to Holly Tree's neat garden.

"It's so weird, you'd never even know there was another cottage there," Ciara said as they headed over to Molly's stables to fetch a couple of brooms.

"I know," Molly said. "It's kind of sad."

They grabbed the brushes and

stopped by the fence to say hello to Niblet and Ranger. The donkey seemed unphased by the dreary weather, but Ranger looked downright put out by the rain, despite his rug. Molly giggled.

"He hates this," she said.

"So do I," Ciara muttered and they laughed.

Grandad, Branden, and Luke had cleared a lot of the doorway with the help of some clippers and brute force by the time they got back. Mum was stood to one side with Maddy and Kit, keeping the pair out of the way, she smiled at them as they headed into the little open-fronted barn and began sweeping out the dirt and dust.

They quickly swept down the walls, knocking off cobwebs and patches of dust, while avoiding the rickety-looking partition. To Ciara's surprise when they started sweeping the floor they found a nice, well-laid flagstone floor in the barn, under what looked like decades of dirt. It was dry though, so it didn't take too long to clear.

"This will be perfect for all the equipment," Molly said as they swept the last bit of the floor clear.

"We're in," Grandad said. "Come on folks."

They trooped into the little cottage following Grandad. Ciara had expected to find a wreck, somewhere that looked abandoned and dilapidated, but the cottage didn't look that bad. The wooden floor was bare, but she could tell it had once been nice and could be again with some work. To one side of her, there was a large open room with windows at either end that would let in a lot of light, if the windows were clean and ivy-free. The furthest wall had a large fireplace in it fitted with the biggest woodburner Ciara had ever seen.

"Does the fire work Dad?" Mum asked.

Grandad nodded. "Yep, had the chimney swept not too long before you moved in, so it should be ok, but they'll need wood for it."

He flicked a switch and the bare lightbulb in the ceiling flicked on. "There's electricity then," Branden said.

"It isn't the dark ages," Grandad chuckled. With the light on it was clear to see the dust laying on the floor and window sills. The walls were bare and patchy in parts.

"This plaster doesn't look too bad," Mum said. "It just needs painting really."

"Let's take a look at the kitchen, we'd best run the taps a bit I reckon, flush them out," Grandad said.

He took them across the little hallway to a neat little kitchen. Its window was completely covered in greenery, so much that in the dimness,

Ciara could barely make out the sink. Grandad flicked the light on and it buzzed to life. Once again Ciara was surprised. The kitchen was small and neat but well laid out with pine cupboard doors and a nice grey sink. There were dark green tiles around the wall behind it and some sort of green/grey stone work surfaces. Grandad turned the tap on and after a few gurgling sounds water spluttered out of them. It looked a little muddy for a second but soon cleared.

"There's hot water too if we turn the boiler on," Grandad said. "I seem to remember it's in one of the cupboards."

They fanned out and opened the

cupboard doors, they were grubby and dusty inside, but not as bad as Ciara had thought they'd be. Maddy let out a little yell as a spider darted from one of them and Kit tried to chase it.

"There's a fridge," Branden said, pulling open a cupboard door.

"Ah, yes, best plug that in Branden, the plug will be in the next-door cupboard," Grandad said. "Ooop, here's the fella," Grandad said, pulling open a cupboard, he fiddled with the old boiler, flicking a few things. "Ah, doesn't look like she wants to fire up. Might have to just boil water for a wash. You want to see the rest or tidy up room by room?" he said, closing the door.

"See the rest," they all seemed to chime at once. Grandad smiled.

The rest of the cottage was in a similar state. There was a large bedroom with no furniture in it at all, though there was a big cupboard built into one wall. The plaster walls were unpainted and dull greyish/pink, and the floor was completely bare. Next to it was the bathroom, it was tiled in horrible pink tiles all over, while the bath, sink, and toilet were all a deep sage green.

"Wow," Mum said. "I'm not sure which is the worst colour."

"It hurts my eyes," Branden said. Luke made a muffled chuckling sound.

"Funny," Grandad said. "Flush the

loo, see if it works while I run the taps."

"I want to flush!" Maddy said, darting forward and pulling the little silver handle on the toilet. It gurgled and then seemed to work. Maddy giggled.

"It's not too bad at all Dad," Mum was saying. "I mean the bathroom needs doing out completely and the boilers shot, but the rest just wants painting. Why doesn't Davie get someone in to finish it off and get it rented?"

Grandad paused, looking a little sheepish. "Ah, well, see Yew Tree isn't really Davies to sort," he said looking at his hands. "Not completely anyway."

"What does that mean?" Ciara asked.

Grandad sighed and sat down on the side of the old green bath. "Well, see your Mum, your Gran, when she passed away I was a bit at a loss. I was over at Davies and we knew the cottages were for sale and he didn't want them being sold and developed and I wanted something to take my mind off things so we sort of decided over a few brandies to buy them together."

"Wait, you mean you own Yew Tree and Holly Tree too?" Ciara asked.

"Oh no," Grandad shook his head. "Holly Tree is all Davies, he just didn't have quite enough to buy both, so I chipped in and bought most of Yew Tree. We did Holly Tree up together and we were starting on Yew Tree when Davie had his stroke. I tried to keep going, but, well I got side-tracked a bit and then you all moved in and..." He threw his hands up.

"You should have said," Mum said with a smile. "We could have helped you."

"Ah, we had other stuff to do," Grandad muttered.

"Well, we know now," she stood up and looked around herself. Ciara recognised the look in her eyes, she was taking charge and that was final. "Right, Ciara, Molly, you two start sweeping and clearing out the living room and the bedroom. Maddy and I will clean the kitchen. Dad, you, Branden, and Luke go out and clear the ivy from around the windows," Branden groaned and Mum shot a glance at him. "Once that's done at least the wreck team can stay here. After that, we can get the walls painted, sort the bathroom and boiler and she'll look as good as new."

Just in time for Davie to sell up Ciara thought to herself. She frowned. No, if Grandad owned some of the cottage too then Davie was much less likely to do that. Mum was already grabbing some of the cleaning things they'd brought and headed to the kitchen with Maddy and Kit in tow.

Molly smiled and held her broom up. Ciara giggled. "This isn't the sort of broom I had in mind running up to Halloween," she said.

"Me either," Molly said, she climbed astride the broom as if it were a hobby horse and headed towards the bedroom with Ciara following laughing.

The bedroom was pretty easy to sweep out, there were a few cobwebs and spiders, especially in the cupboard, but on the whole, it was more just layers of dust on the floor. Ciara looked around when they'd finished and smiled. She'd been expecting mould and damp and blown plaster. This, she thought, was pretty nice.

"It's a shame there's only one bedroom," Molly said leaning on her brush.

"I suppose you could turn the little barn on the side into another one," she thought aloud.

Molly shook her head. "It shares a wall with the kitchen, no one is going to want to walk through the kitchen to go to bed."

"Branden might," Ciara mused. "It'd be close for midnight snacks."

They laughed and headed towards the living room. The dust here was thicker and there were more cobwebs. They began by clearing off the wide window sills and the huge beam across the fireplace.

"This fire is amazing," Molly said, stroking the beam.

"It really is," Ciara said with a smile. She imagined what it would be like all lit up and warm. It was like something you saw in a magazine at Christmas.

They had just about finished sweeping up when Mum and Maddy appeared from the kitchen. Grandad, Luke, and Branden had cleared the ivy from the window and it looked a lot brighter. It certainly was a cleaner, Mum had scrubbed and polished the doors and the stone top until they shone.

"Well, it's certainly looking a bit better," Mum said.

"I think it's lovely," Ciara said. Mum smiled. "Right, let's go get some tea shall we, I think we've earned it."

Ciara glanced at her watch. It had a little cartoon horse on it, his tail pointing to the hour. She was surprised to see it was so late. "It'll be dark soon, we need to get the horses in."

"You two go ahead, get them in, we'll gather the stuff up and meet you at home," Mum said with a smile.

Ciara and Molly smiled and darted off. They put the brushes back in Molly's little tack room and brought in Ranger and Niblet first. Ranger almost ran into his stable, keen to get into the warm and dry. Molly shook her head at him as she undid his headcollar and fetched his feed bucket.

The rain had stopped by the time they headed up the drive to Grandad's. Big puddles had formed all along the driveway, they shimmered a little in the autumn sun and rippled when the golden leaves fell into them.

"It might be ok for a ride tomorrow," Molly said with a smile.

Ciara nodded. "The beauty of riding on the beach is that the sand doesn't get muddy," she smiled.

Molly opened up all the stable doors while Ciara caught Misty and led her inside. Her neck started to steam as soon as she was in the stable.

"Misty's misty," Molly giggled.

They fetched the boys next, Molly taking Aramis and Ciara bringing the less sensible, but just as large Louie. Both geldings fell on their hay as soon as they were let loose.

"Someone's hungry," Molly said as she closed Aramis's door.

"Yeah, there's not much on the paddock now. We're going to swap them over in a few days," Ciara smiled. Grandad had pretty much agreed with Davie to buy the back field now. He was planning on using it in the summer months for the sheep, that way the horses could have the large field the sheep had been using in the summer and two paddocks in the winter. The idea made Ciara smile. She thought

Misty and the boys would like that very much.

"Speaking of hungry," Molly said, nodding in the direction of the house. Ciara smiled. She was starving, she wondered what Mum had for tea. They headed around to grab the horse's feeds and were just putting the buckets in when Grandad's car pulled up and everyone piled out.

"Leave the cleaning stuff in the car," Mum said. "We'll get it later on."

"Sounds good to me," Grandad said with a smile.

"Right, I'll go sort the dinner. I put a casserole on before we went, it should be perfect about now," Mum said. "Ten minutes." She headed indoors with Grandad, Maddy, and Kit, but instead of following them, Branden and Luke came over to the stables.

"We have an idea," Branden said leaning on Misty's door.

"About what?" Ciara asked.

Branden smiled. "About the cottage. You know when we moved in we helped Grandad do the place up a bit?"

Ciara nodded, Grandad's house had been a little dated when they moved in and Branden had helped him paint the place, including her and Maddy's bedroom.

"Well," Branden went on. "There's a ton of paint left. We, Luke and I, thought we could paint out the living room and the bedroom, make it look nice as a surprise. You want to help?"

Molly and Ciara looked at each other with a smile. Grandad was always helping people, it would be nice to help him for a change. Ciara nodded.

"Cool," Branden grinned. "We're going down in the morning."

"We could ride early," Ciara said looking at Molly. "Then I could say I'm going over to yours to sort out more of our Halloween costumes or something."

Molly nodded. "Ok, I'll tell Mum what's going on so she can cover for us. Let's ride about 8ish, it'll be light then."

"Ok, we'll aim to meet at the cove at about 8.15." Ciara nodded.

"And I'll snag some bits from Dad's workshop," Luke said. "He won't mind, he always says I can take what I want so long as I put it back. There might even be some old stock we can have kicking about out there. I'll ask tonight."

"This is going to be epic!" Branden said excitedly.

Chapter 7

The sun was up and shining when Ciara and Misty wandered down the lane to meet Molly and Ranger. She was looking forward to their ride before heading over to help Branden and Luke. She'd told Grandad they were getting out while the weather was alright. She hoped he believed her. Molly waved at her as she headed into the dunes and Ciara waved back, Misty whickering at Ranger.

"Hey," Ciara called.

"Hi," Molly said. "This is a bit better."

"I know," Ciara smiled. They headed down to the beach chatting happily.

It was Misty who first spotted the person out in the sea. She stopped short halfway across the sand and stared out over the choppy water. The weather had calmed a lot, but the sea was still rougher than it had been during the summer months.

"What is it?" Ciara asked Misty. She followed the mare's gaze out over the water. Ciara squinted, something was bobbing about not too far from the wreck. "What is that?" she said pointing. Molly looked out and gasped.

"I think it's a person," Molly said, frowning. "Do you think they're from the wreck team? I didn't think they were coming tomorrow."

"They are," Ciara said confused. She tried to see the figure better, whoever it was they didn't seem to be moving.

Unsure what else to do, they instinctively rode towards the sea to get a closer look, neither one saying a word. As they drew closer Ciara could see that the figure was waving a hand, bobbing around in the surf, their head and arms being swamped at times.

Ciara looked over at Molly in horror. Her heart began to race. "I think they're in trouble," she said.

"What do we do?" Molly asked, almost as frantic.

For a second Ciara looked out over the sea, her mind racing. Were they really watching someone out in the sea drowning? Who were they? What were they doing in the cove at this time of the morning?

"We should get help," Molly said, turning Ranger around.

Ciara paused as the figure dipped down more than they had before. She wasn't sure that whoever they were had time for them to ride for help. She swallowed hard, her mind racing. In her heart, she knew whoever this was would be drowned before someone could run down and help.

"You go," Ciara said. "Go, get your Dad." She urged Misty towards the sea.

"What are you doing!" Molly yelled in horror.

Ciara turned in her saddle. "We're the only chance they have," she said. "Misty's way stronger in the water than any of us. I can drag the person back in."

"No," Molly said. "No! It's too dangerous, what if you get pulled off or something."

"We can't just watch them drown! I'll only go as far out as the edge of the sandbank, Misty won't even be swimming. Go get your Dad fast," Ciara said. "GO!"

Molly spun Ranger around on his hind legs. The chestnut Arab seemed to sense the tension in the air. All trace of the spookiness that sometimes accompanied his temperament was suddenly gone and Ciara realised for the first time that he 'put on' his 'oh that's so scary' moments, rather than actually being afraid. He charged over the sand faster than Ciara had ever seen him move, his tail streaming, his ears pricked. If there hadn't been someone in trouble, it would have been an impressive sight.

Ciara turned back to the sea and took a deep breath. Her heart was pounding and she couldn't quite believe she was about to do what she was thinking of doing. She shoved thoughts of the danger to herself and Misty aside. Pulling down her stirrup leather she made it as long as she could, remembering to flick the little peg of her stirrup bar up. She swallowed hard. They had always been told to leave the bar straight so that if they fell off the leather would pull free from the saddle, it seemed wrong to alter it, but she needed the leather to stay in place this time. Ciara glanced out at the sea determinedly and urged the bay mare forwards. Misty didn't hesitate for a second.

They had been going in the sea on and off for a while now. Grandad had taken them out almost as far as the figure was a couple of times, but the weather had been warm and bright and they were always supervised. The bay had a long sandy shelf that they could ride right out on without the horses needing to swim, though it got pretty deep. If Ciara was right the figure in the water was just off the edge of it, at least that's what she hoped.

Misty splashed through the little waves and into the sea. As the water crept up over Ciara's legs she shivered. It was cold, really cold. Misty didn't seem to notice much, her thick coat was certainly helpful now, but Ciara could feel the chill creeping up her whole body. No wonder whoever it was out there was in trouble.

Misty surged forward through the

waves, pushing herself through the water that crept higher and higher on her. Ciara kept an eye on the swimmer, hoping they could hold on, if they went under the water before Ciara and Misty reached them, there would be nothing Ciara could do. She swallowed hard, willing the figure to keep going.

Soon enough the water was up to Misty's shoulders. When they had waded before it had been fun, splashing in the coolness on baking days. Now though it was different. Ciara pushed the numbing cold from her mind and focused on the figure. Grandad had said that horses often liked being in the water, but that they couldn't see well. They needed direction or they could swim right out to sea and not be able to get back, that's why he told them only to wade and to always keep a good contact. The thought of the Spanish horses swimming from the wrecked ship suddenly jumped into Ciara's head unbidden, but she pushed the thought away.

It seemed to be taking forever to get to the figure in the water and with every movement of Misty's legs Ciara felt her panic rising. Could they do this? She worried Misty would tire out herself and need rescuing too, or that she'd get so cold she couldn't help either herself or the figure. The waves lapped higher on her legs, the cold almost making Ciara want to cry. Salty splashes of cold water hit her face. Not too far, she told herself, we can do this, we can do this. She said it over and over as they slowly crossed the bay.

Finally, the figure was close enough for Ciara to see clearly. It was a boy, and not just any boy. It was Russel Grant from school. Ciara pushed her shock at seeing Russel aside. He was pale, almost to the point of looking blue. She wondered if she looked that cold. Misty was almost at him now. There was a wild panicked look in his eyes as he bobbed up and down, clawing at the surface of the water desperate not to go down. It was like he was scrabbling for something solid and not finding it. The image burnt itself into Ciara's mind.

Ciara wondered if Russel knew she was there. Branden had done his lifesaving course at a swimming class a summer before and Ciara tried to think back to what he had said. He'd insisted on teaching both her and Maddy a few things and suddenly she was very glad he had. Branden said often someone in trouble would swamp a rescuer, not aware of what they were doing, just looking for something to latch onto to stop them going under. Ciara was pretty sure Russel couldn't swamp Misty, but he could pull her off if she wasn't careful.

"Russel, Russel," she called over the sounds of the waves. After another attempt, he looked at her his eyes wide and frantic. "I'm going to help, but you need to do what I say, ok?" She was pretty sure he couldn't speak, but he seemed to nod. "Ok." She pulled her foot free from her stirrup and urged Misty closer. She knew they were right at the edge of the sand bar, too much further and they'd fall into the dip. "Catch the stirrup," she said, throwing it out towards him. "We'll pull you in."

It took Russel two attempts to catch hold of the stirrup leather, and for a second Ciara worried he was too cold to hold on. Finally, though he seemed to catch it, he looped his arm through the leather and Ciara turned Misty back towards the beach.

Slowly they began to swim towards home, pulling Russel with them. Ciara could feel Misty was getting a little tired now, but she strode out still. The cold was so intense now that Ciara was feeling almost sleepy. She wondered how long Russel had been out there, it couldn't have been long.

Ciara looked up at the beach and realised she could see Ranger. Beside him, running almost as fast as the horse was trotting, was a figure, a second one was running after it. Tom, Ciara thought with relief, and Faye.

Misty's foot hit solid ground and Ciara heaved a sigh of relief. They splashed through the water heading closer and closer to the beach. Suddenly Tom was beside them, hauling Russel from the stirrup and dragging him through the breaking waves. Free of extra weight, Misty walked more happily ashore. As soon as they were on the firm sand, Ciara slid off her. Faye was next to her in a flash, wrapping her in a blanket.

"Misty," she said through chattering teeth. She realised her fingers were numb and that she had barely felt the reins.

"I got her," Molly's voice came from behind them. "She's ok, a bit cold."

"Come on, everyone to the house," Faye said. "Paramedics are on the way."

"I got the boy," Tom said, scooping Russel up in his arms and heading toward the sand.

They began to walk over the sand. They hadn't gotten far when Branden and Luke appeared running over the sand.

"Here," Luke said, taking one side of Ciara, while Branden got the other.

"We got her," Branden said. Faye nodded and went to help Tom with Russel. "What the hell!" Branden said.

Ciara shivered. "You could have been killed." She glanced at Russel.

"Thanks," she said, shivering. "I remembered what you said, about rescuing people."

Branden shook his head. "Don't ever do this again!"

"I'll try," she shivered.

The paramedics were pulling into Holly Tree Cottage as they came up the little track. They took Russel into the back of the ambulance straight away and covered him in blankets, taking vital signs and hooking him up to machines. One of the paramedics wrapped a silver blanket around Ciara and took her to one side to check over, but she was more worried about Misty. Molly put her in Niblet's stable and rubbed her dry with a towel, giving her a large net and wrapping her up in one of Ranger's rugs.

Mum, Grandad, and Maddy arrived a few minutes later. Mum looked furious but seeing Russel lying in the ambulance her face softened. Grandad just looked relieved. He came over and pulled Ciara into a hug.

"What were you thinking?" he asked.

"I didn't want him to drown," Ciara managed a lot more clearly. "How's Misty?"

"I'll check her," Grandad said, leaving Ciara with Branden and Mum.

"I don't know whether to be proud or angry," Mum said. Ciara smiled a little and Mum pulled her into a hug.

The paramedic came around the side of the ambulance looking serious. "We won't need to take her in, she's ok," the woman smiled. "But she needs to rest up today and stay warm."

"What about Russel?" Ciara asked.

"That's his name?"

Ciara nodded. "Russel Grant. He goes to my school."

"He's stable, but he's not out of the woods. Do you know what he was doing in the cove, how long he'd been there?" she asked.

Ciara shook her head. "No, we just spotted him in the sea."

"Ok," the woman said with a nod. She turned away and closed the back doors of the ambulance. The engine roared to life and it pulled away, it flashed its lights and turned on the siren when it reached the road. Ciara stared after it confused by everything that had just happened. They were supposed to have a quiet ride on the beach, not a rescue mission.

Faye ushered everyone inside, promising to drive Ciara home after she'd warmed up a little. Cira followed her reluctantly glancing towards the stable Misty was in as she walked through the door. Tom stoked the fire in the living room before going to change his wet clothes, and Ciara found herself sitting by the warm flames wrapped in a blanket.

Grandad came in just as Faye handed her a mug of hot sweet tea. Ciara looked up at him fearfully, worried he was going to say Misty was in trouble or needed a vet. He smiled at her.

"She's fine, Molly did a good job drying her off and she's toasty now. We'll keep an eye on her just like we are with you, and maybe keep her in with a good net today. All in all, though I'd say the pair of you got off lightly," he said. Ciara let out a huge sigh of relief. All of a sudden she felt very tired.

"What on earth was he doing out

there, that's what I want to know," Faye said. Ciara noticed her hands were shaking just a little.

Mum shook her head. "I wonder if his parents know. Oh, can you imagine?"

Tom jogged down the stairs in dry clothes and came over checking Ciara and then Molly. He smiled at them. "I think we'll have to hire you two."

"No chance," Mum said.

Tom smiled. "Where did you learn that rescue technique?" he asked.

Ciara smiled shyly and looked at her mug. "Grandad's been taking us into the sea to ride. I knew we could get there. Branden told me how to rescue a swimmer."

Everyone, including Luke, looked at Branden. He held his hands up. "I just passed on what I learnt at the Lifesavers course at the pool, I didn't expect them to put it into practice."

"Them?" Mum asked.

Branden glanced at Maddy who was sitting quietly on a chair by the window. Mum sighed and then smiled.

"Well, I'm very proud of all of you," Mum said.

"We all are," Grandad put in. "Molly did a great job getting help fast, Branden, Luke you did a good job helping get everyone back here and Ciara, you, I think deserve a very, very big thank you from that young lad."

Ciara smiled a little, but she

wondered if Russel would be able to give her that thank you. Sure, they'd pulled him out, but the paramedic said he wasn't out of the woods yet. She couldn't help but think what might have happened if they hadn't ridden early. What if Branden hadn't wanted to help Grandad and asked her and Molly to chip in? It would have been so easy for them not to be there, to not see Russel. He'd have been missing and she would probably never have known he was out there in the cove somewhere. The thought made her shudder and think about all the sailors who had perished on the wreck itself. At least they made it, she thought to herself, another horse had swum ashore from the ship now, but this one had brought two people safely with her. Misty was definitely a hero.

Chapter 8

Misty snuffled around in Ciara's pocket hopefully. Ciara giggled and pulled out another carrot passing it to her. Grandad had walked Misty back from Molly's together with Branden and Lucas, half an hour before, while Mum had driven Ciara and Maddy. Ciara had still felt shaken but a lot better by the time they trooped to the car. Faye had insisted Ciara and Misty stay put for a few hours until they were thawed out and dry.

Ciara had warmed up slowly by the fire, feeling the numbing cold slowly give way to tiredness. She wondered if Misty had felt the same. The little bay mare hadn't shown any signs of fatigue. She'd stood shivering a little and stuffing her mouth with Ranger's hay, steam rising from her damp coat. Grandad kept popping out and checking on her, the third time he reported back that she was no longer shivering and was drying off pretty quickly. Ciara had felt relieved. That in itself had made her feel even more exhausted.

Once she had recovered a bit, she found herself telling everyone what had happened again as they tried to piece together what had gone on. No one could think of a reason for Russel to have been out swimming in the bay, especially since he'd been wearing his clothes. Ciara hadn't noticed what he was wearing and it came as a bit of a shock to her that she'd pulled him out in trousers and a jumper.

"He was mighty lucky," Tom had said. "Those clothes could have dragged him down."

Branden had nodded. "He mustn't have been out there very long." Tom agreed.

"You think he went in for a swim?" Lucas asked. "Or, well, I mean, I could see him falling in being more likely."

Ciara hadn't thought of that. She realised she hadn't really thought about how or why Russel was there at all, the only thing that had crossed her mind was to fish him out quickly before he drowned. Still, thinking now she thought Lucas was probably right. Russel had probably wandered out onto the black rocks, trying to look at the wreck she guessed. Grandad had said it was slippery when they had been down there with Ruth and Ian. She pictured Russel scrambling over the wet rocks, maybe he slipped, maybe a big wave caught him, but still, he ended up in the water splashing around. Yeah, that definitely seemed much more likely than him jumping in fully clothed for a swim. Ciara shuddered. Branden was right, with his heavy clothes on he would be dragged down quickly, he really was lucky.

Misty finished the carrot and sniffed about for another. Ciara held her hands up with a smile and Misty looked at her for a few seconds. Seeing the carrots were gone, she lent in and rubbed her head on Ciara before turning to grab some more hay. She seemed to be enjoying her duvet day. Ciara smiled. She had been sent inside as soon as they got home, but had pestered Mum until she'd allowed her to go and check on Misty in her own stable. Now she had seen with her own eyes that Misty was fine, she felt a mix of relief and exhaustion. She sat down on an upturned bucket by the door, watching as Misty ate her hay. Her mind wandered from the events of the day to Grandad. All thoughts of sorting out the cottage had gone out of the window thanks to Russel.

"Knock knock." Ciara looked up to see Branden standing by the stable door. Misty looked at him hopefully, but when he didn't produce anything of interest to eat, she turned back to the net.

"You ok?" Branden asked. Ciara nodded. "And she's ok?"

Misty looked back at him and snorted. Ciara giggled and nodded again. Branden smiled.

"Sorry we didn't get the cottage done," Ciara said.

"What?" Branden shook his head. "You saved a boy from drowning and you're sorry you couldn't help paint?"

Ciara wrinkled her nose, when he put it like that it did seem like a silly thing to say. Branden smiled again, he leaned over the door a little more.

"Besides, it's not off," he whispered conspiratorially. "Lucas and I are going down there now, we'll make a start. Any chance you could find a way to keep Grandad out of the way for a bit? If you're up to it, that is?"

Ciara smiled and nodded. "Actually, I was thinking about asking to go and see Russel, make sure he's ok. Maybe I could get Grandad to take me."

"Perfect," Branden said. He turned and then stopped and looked back. "You know you guys are heroes, right? I mean, you did something super brave today, stupid, but super brave." He walked away leaving Ciara alone, she could feel her cheeks burning a little as she blushed. It seemed wrong to be called a hero or brave for doing what you thought was right. Misty didn't seem to mind though, if anything Ciara thought she was enjoying being the centre of attention.

It took a while to persuade Grandad to take her down to see Russel. He kept telling her she'd be better off going tomorrow after a good night's sleep, but eventually, Ciara wore him down. Mum had made her promise not to be too long and to only go in if the doctors or nurses said it was alright.

The hospital was just outside of the closest town, not far from school. Grandad had pulled up in the car park and glanced at the jumble of rectangle buildings with a sigh. They looked, he had said, like some sort of institution, all clinical and uninviting. Ciara had pointed out that it was almost all of those things and Grandad rolled his eyes. He said when he was young the hospital had been a nice stone-built building with character, not like this '70s monstrosity. Ciara had smiled.

They had walked across the car park in silence. Every step made Ciara realise how tired she was, but she really did want to see Russel, making sure he was alright would, she felt, let her go home and sleep happily.

Inside the hospital, they found a little reception desk. The lady behind it was on the phone and they waited patiently until she was finished. She glanced up as she hung up the receiver.

"Can I help you?" she asked.

Grandad took a deep breath and then frowned as if unsure of where to start. He looked at Ciara. "Bit complicated," he said and then smiled at the receptionist. "See, my granddaughter here, she pulled a boy out of the sea with her pony this morning and..."

The nurse cut him off. "That was you?" she looked at Ciara. "Oh, we've heard all about it, you and that pony of yours saving that poor lad." Ciara blushed.

"Yes," Grandad said with a cough. "Thing is, well, we were just wondering if there was any chance we could see him, check he's alright." He lent in a little. "I think it would make Ciara feel a bit better to know he wasn't in any danger."

The lady nodded, she smiled over at Ciara. "He's on the pediatric ward, second floor, third corridor on the right. I'll call up and let them know you're coming. I don't know if he can have visitors, but if nothing else I'm sure someone can tell you how he's doing."

"Thank you," Grandad said with a smile.

They followed the lady's directions, taking the lift up to the second floor and following the signs for the ward. The little door that led to it had a push button lock on the outside and a little speaker box with a buzzer under it. Grandad pushed the button and a few seconds later there was a crackle from the speaker.

"Oh, hi," Grandad said. "It's em,

it's Ciara to see that boy that fell in the sea."

"Russel," Ciara piped up. "Russel Grant."

"Come in," a scratchy voice said through the box. A second later there was a buzz and a click announcing that the door had been unlocked. Grandad swung the door open and they trooped into the ward.

Ciara hadn't been in many hospitals, and she'd only seen wards on TV, but the ones she had seen always looked bright and stark, this one, however, looked much more fun. The walls had been painted with cartoon characters and the little side bays all had toys and TVs in them. Ciara walked along following Grandad, she glanced into one of the little bays and a boy looking out waved at her, she waved back with a smile.

The nurse's station seemed busy, but a nice nurse with long black hair fastened in a myriad of thin plaits, smiled at them as they walked up.

"You must be Ciara the hero," she said with a grin. Ciara blushed again; she was beginning to dislike being called that. She shrugged. "You want to make sure your friend is ok, yes?" Ciara wasn't sure she'd call Russel her friend, but she nodded all the same. The nurse looked from side to side. "We're not supposed to have visitors right now, but, well, you did pull him out of the sea, so, come on."

She stood up and led them further into the ward to a small side room. Ciara guessed that since they were being taken to see him, that Russel must be alright on the whole. They stopped by the door and the nurse knocked, pushing it open a little and poking her head in.

"Wait here a second," she said and slipped inside, closing the door behind her.

A few minutes later she returned with a smile. "Ok, you can go in, but make it quick, he's still pretty tired out."

"I'll wait here for you," Grandad said, taking up position by the door.

Ciara smiled. She reached out and took hold of the cold metal door handle and began to slowly push it down. As she did, the memories of being out in the sea flooded her mind for a moment. This time it was less the freezing, biting cold that threatened to dull the feelings in her legs and hands, and more the panic. The fear in Russel's eyes and the pounding of her own heart. She swallowed hard and pushed open the door.

Russel was laid in a little hospital bed, the only one in the room. Its pale blue walls made the room feel cool and Ciara shivered despite the warmth. She walked across the linoleum-covered floor and stood by the bed. Russel turned his head on the pillow to look at her. She had to admit he looked a lot better than the last times she had seen him, but his face still seemed paler than usual and there were dark rims under his brown eyes.

"Hey," he said with a slight, lopsided smile.

"Hi," Ciara said.

There was a moment of awkward silence before he cleared his throat. "Thanks for pulling me out," he said.

Ciara suddenly laughed and a second later Russel started laughing too before it made him cough.

"Stop," he said. "Laughing makes me cough."

They fell into silence again, but Ciara still smiled. "You're welcome, by the way," Ciara said with a smirk.

Russel smiled and Ciara sat down in the chair by the bedside. "What's the horse called?" he asked suddenly.

Ciara grinned. "Misty," she said. "Her name's Misty."

"Can you thank her too?" he asked. This time neither of them laughed. Ciara nodded. "You two, you're ok, right?"

"Yeah," Ciara said. "Just cold." She saw Russel shudder. Neither of them was going to forget that cold feeling any time soon she thought. "Why were you out there?" Ciara asked suddenly.

Russel looked down at the white sheet on his bed for a minute. "It was an accident."

"I thought that," Ciara said. "I figured you'd gone out on the rocks to look at the wreck and either slipped or been washed in."

Russel looked a little ashamed. "Washed in," he said quietly.

"Why though?" Ciara asked. "I mean, I know the wreck's cool, but you can see it pretty well from the beach."

Russel sighed, he glanced at the window and back at Ciara. "Ok, look, if I tell you something, promise you won't laugh." Ciara nodded. She expected he'd been dared by one of his friends, but looking at his face she suddenly thought there was something else. "Years ago, my Grandad told me this story about a Spanish wreck, it was part of the armada and sunk. Anyway, years later it appeared after a storm, pushed closer to the beach. Some smugglers found it and took stuff from it, hiding it in a cave on the shore close by. On the last trip they took to it, the smuggler's boat suffered the same fate, sinking by the wreck. There was one survivor, my ancestor, Bart Grant. The story's been in the family for years, but no one really believed it, except Grandad and, well me. When the wreck washed up, I figured the cave must be in the rocks by Coral Cove and I wanted to check it out and prove Grandad was right, that it was real." Russel looked at his hands. "My Grandad passed away last year." Ciara heard his voice hitch.

"Why didn't you just tell the wreck team?" Ciara asked.

Russel looked at her with a frown. "What, tell them a story that no one believes except me."

"I believe it," Ciara said quietly. Russel shot her a look, and Ciara smiled. "My Grandad told me a similar story, he said it was a local legend."

Russel bit his lip and looked around the room. "Can you get my trousers from the cupboard over there?" he said, nodding towards a tall wooden cupboard on one wall by the

TV.

Ciara stood up and walked over pulling open the door. Inside were a pair of black trousers and a grey jumper, still slightly damp.

"Look in the pocket, the right one," Russel said.

Ciara pushed her hand into the pocket. Her fingers closed around something hard and cold almost the size of her palm. She pulled it out and looked down at her hand. A gasp escaped her. She closed the door and hurried back over to Russel still clutching the golden coin in her hand. He smiled at her.

"It's a doubloon, I know it is, it's from the cave or the wreck. I found it on the rocks just before I was washed in," he said.

"It's amazing," Ciara said looking at it.

"You take it," he said. Ciara looked up quickly and he smiled. "Tell the wreck team about it and my Grandad's story. It's proof, at least a bit of proof."

"I can't take this!" Ciara said.

"Yeah," Russel said, putting his head back on the pillow. "You can."

Chapter 9

Ciara sat in her room looking out of her window at the sun slowly sinking in the sky. She turned the doubloon over in her fingers, the sunlight glinting off the golden metal. The wreck team had arrived early that morning and she'd been keen to go down and show them Russel's coin, but she'd not had the chance. Mum was watching her like a hawk after her and Misty's adventures the day before, she had been given strict instructions to have an easy day, as was Misty. Ciara sighed. She'd finally shown Grandad the coin and begged him to take her down to meet the team, but he'd shook his head.

"I'll take you down first thing in the morning though," he'd smiled. "Branden says there's some sort of surprise down there he wants me to see anyway. We'll take Misty, have an easy walk."

Ciara had smiled, she knew all about Branden's surprise of course. The wreck team had turned up while they were visiting Russel the evening before and Branden had insisted on taking them down to Yew Tree and letting them in. The team had been very grateful to have the cottage as a place to stay. He'd told her later that night that he and Lucas had managed to paint the living room out and put a few bits of old carpet from the garage down like rugs, she wondered what it looked like. Ciara yawned, she supposed she'd find out tomorrow.

It was barely dawn when Ciara woke up. Maddy was asleep, one arm wrapped around Kit, who seemed to be sleeping with her more and more. Ciara fished the doubloon out from under her pillow and hurried to get dressed. She knew Grandad would be up already, he always got up with the sun as he put it.

She bounced down the stairs and into the kitchen to find Grandad putting a plate of buttered muffins on the table. She smiled.

"How did you know I was up?" she asked.

"How did I know? Well, it was either you or a herd of elephants," he smirked. Ciara grinned and took a large bite from the muffin.

"Can we go to Yew Tree straight after breakfast?" she asked.

Grandad chuckled. "Oh why not," he said. "The team's likely up, they said they'd be working long hours as long as the weather holds to get done. I daresay they'll want to hear about Russel and that coin too."

"Do you know what they did yesterday?" Ciara asked around a

mouthful of toasty yumminess.

"As far as I know they just set up all their equipment and assessed the site," Grandad said. Ciara nodded.

As soon as they had finished eating, Ciara darted outside to get Misty ready and Grandad turned out Aramis and Louie. Mum was up just in time to see Ciara hop onto the mounting block and wave goodbye. She shook her head and then shrugged and waved back.

Misty ambled along beside Grandad as if the events of the other day had never happened. Ciara had been worried she wouldn't want to head towards the cove, that being in the cold water would put her off, but she seemed to understand that it was a one-off event. An emergency that was not to be repeated. They walked up from the dunes past Holly Tree and Ciara paused to say hi to Molly, Ranger, and Niblet. She showed Molly the doubloon too.

"Ooh," she said. "Can I take a better look later?"

"Why don't you come by for tea," Grandad said. "Laura's making a special supper both in honour of you two rescuing Russel and so we can invite the wreck team over. She doesn't reckon they can cook properly in Yew Tree with it being a bit of a shell. There isn't really an oven."

"Ok," Molly said. "I'll tell Mum."

Molly raced off to speak to her mum, while Grandad and Ciara walked onward towards Yew Tree cottage. It was certainly more visible now with most of the ivy removed or cut back. There was a woman outside by the little barn, putting things in an inflatable boat. She waved when she saw them coming.

"Hi," she called.

"Hello," Grandad replied. "I'm Pat, are you part of the team?"

The lady smiled. "Yeah, my name's Mandy, nice to meet you." She shook Grandad's hand. "And you must be Ciara," she turned towards Misty and Ciara, Ciara nodded. "And who are you?" she asked, fussing at Misty. The bay mare nuzzled at Mandy's pockets.

"This is Misty," Ciara said.

"Ah," Mandy smiled. "The hero pony." Ciara grinned. "I have a horse, Dixie." She kept petting Misty. "My friend's looking after her while I'm here."

Ciara was just going to ask more about Mandy's horse when Ruth and Ian emerged from the cottage. "Morning," Ian said with a smile.

"Morning," Grandad replied. "You settle in ok?"

"Yes, thanks," Ruth said. "Much warmer and drier than a tent."

"No oven though," Grandad said.

"Well, sandwiches were nice," Ruth said.

"Still, we'd like you all to come up to the house tonight, Laura thought you might like a warm dinner," Grandad said with a smile.

"Oh, well, thanks very much," Ian said. "Much appreciated."

"We best get down to the wreck," Ruth said, nudging Ian's arm. "I'll get Jim and we can head over."

"Wait," Ciara said as she turned to go. Ruth paused and looked back at her. Ciara slid down from Misty and pulled the doubloon out of her pocket, she pushed the coin into Ruth's hand without saying anything. Ruth looked at it and gasped, she handed the coin to Ian.

"Now where did you get his?" Ian

asked.

"It's a bit of a story. Russel found it," Ciara said.

"Russel?" Ian asked.

"The young lad she pulled out of the sea yesterday," Grandad said.

"I think you better tell us everything," Ruth said.

It took Ciara quite some time to tell the wreck team, including Jim who joined them, the whole story. Everything from saving Russel to thawing out, to visiting him in the hospital and getting the coin. She even told them his old grandfather's story. Once she had finished, Ian turned the coin over in his hands, one eyebrow raised.

"It's quite a tale," he said.

"Do you think it could be true?" Ciara asked. "About the smugglers and the cave?"

"No telling really," Ian said. "It's possible that the wreck has shifted twice and that someone took stuff off it earlier. Then again, this could have been tossed up on the rocks by a wave," Ian pointed out.

"There are caves there," Grandad chipped in. "I remember seeing them as a kid. We went down there exploring, but my old man caught us, and tanned us good and proper."

"Where was the cave?" Ruth asked. "Could we see it from the sea?"

Grandad shook his head. "Not

unless you knew where to look. It's hidden in a cleft."

"You know," Jim said thoughtfully. "We've got the climbing gear. We could anchor to the rocks and check it out. It might be a good way to look at the ship as well."

"Let's do it," Ruth said. "We'll set up the anchor points and safety lines today, while Ian and Mandy start recording the ship."

"Sounds like a plan," Mandy smiled.

"Well, you'll need to let us know what you find out later," Grandad said. The team agreed. "Oh, Branden asked if I could pop in and see something in the living room. Is that ok?"

"It's your place," Ian said.

"I'll just be a second Ciara," he said and popped inside as the team began to haul their things and the boat toward the beach.

Mandy patted Misty as she left, and she smiled at Ciara. "That's some story you have to tell. I have a good one too, maybe we can swap horse tales later." Ciara beamed and nodded.

She climbed back into the saddle just as Grandad appeared shaking his head. "Your brother is a sneaky one eh?" he smiled. "Did a nice job though."

The rest of the day passed slowly for Ciara. She wanted to go down to the beach and watch the teamwork, but from what they said there wouldn't be much to see. It was too chilly to go play in the playhouse, so she spent a good part of the day doing a puzzle with Maddy.

It was just before tea when the wreck team turned up. They looked cold and a little damp. The shower in Yew Tree cottage wasn't in a great state and while the heating was working, the cottage still hadn't dried out after standing empty for so long. Grandad lit the wood burner in the living room and Mum suggested they all take a shower before dinner was served. No one argued with her.

Many showered first and then sat down by the warmth of the fire helping Ciara and Maddy with the puzzle they had laid out on a board on the floor.

Ciara glanced at her.

"You want *my* horse story don't you," Mandy chuckled, not looking away from the puzzle piece in her hand.

"Kinda," Ciara said, crinkling her nose.

Mandy chuckled. She put the piece in place and sat up a little, the warm glow of the fire illuminating her face. "Well, it was interesting," she smiled. "I told you I had a horse, Dixie," Ciara nodded. "Well, last summer I was one of three adult supervisors on a charity trail ride. You know the sort of thing, you have stop-off points you stay at with your horse and hack between them in stages. It should have been easy, we did the ride, me and Julie my friend, no problems at all," she paused and Ciara looked at her expectantly.

"What went wrong?" Maddy asked her attention now on Mandy and not the puzzle.

"Well, to start with, Julie's horse went lame. That wasn't too bad, he was alright and we still had two adults on the ride. We thought we'd be fine, until," Mandy paused.

"Until?" Ciara prompted.

"A storm blew up, a big one. We could see it coming," Mandy said. "Dixie's pretty good in most things, but not thunder. We tried to outrun it, but the edge of it caught up with us too fast. There was this huge boom,

I've never heard thunder like it before. Dixie, she threw the biggest spook. I tried to stay with her, but there was no way."

"Were you hurt?" Ciara asked.

Mandy nodded. "Yeah, pretty banged up. We weren't sure what to do. I couldn't ride Dixie, I couldn't get on her. She was too big and still too hyped up. And to make things worse, there was no phone signal for miles."

"What did you do?" Ciara asked.

"Well, I was lucky. My friend Lisa, her niece was on the ride. She has this amazing pony called Ozzie. They got me up on him. Lisa rode Dixie and her niece rode Lisa's mare. She wasn't bothered by the storm at all. Anyway, we rode to a little bothy not too far away that one of the kids knew about, how lucky is that? I wasn't sure what we were going to do when we got there though, other than ride out the storm," Mandy said. "The kids were amazing; they saw to the horses and brought everything inside the place." Mandy paused, shaking her head at the memory.

"Did you ride Ozzie all the way to the next stop?" Maddy asked stroking Kit absently, the dog rolled over onto his back for tummy tickles and Maddy smiled.

"No," Mandy shook her head. "No, I couldn't. Lisa wanted to ride out for help, but in the end, the kids did.

They worked as a team and they rode the next stage of the ride. It was amazing. They got help sent up to collect me and my friend, Julie, she's the one looking after Dixie right now, she came and rode her out for me."

"That's so cool," Ciara said.

"It really was," Mandy said. "They're planning on some kind of reunion party this Christmas, the kids, they made an amazing team. A bit like you and your Misty I think having heard your story earlier." Ciara blushed.

Just then the doorbell rang and Maddy scrambled up to go and answer it. Molly, Faye, and Tom trooped in and Mum came out to greet them and offer them all a drink.

It was a jolly party of people that crammed around the table in the kitchen. Grandad had brought in extra chairs from the garage and Mum had put a lot of plates of warm food and nibbles on the table.

"I didn't expect a feast," Jim said with a smile as he filled his plate.

"Did you find anything interesting today?" Grandad asked, taking a bite of a sausage roll.

"Actually, we did," Ruth said. "We found the cave."

"Really?" Ciara asked excitedly.

Ian nodded. "Not explored it yet, but we have safety anchors in place and it's safe to start exploring tomorrow."

"Wow," Ciara said.

"You want to check it out with us?" Jim asked. "If it's ok with your Mum's." He looked from Faye to Mum and back.

Ciara looked appealingly at Mum, she glanced at them and sighed. "Alright, but only Ciara and Branden, Maddy's too young."

"Aww," Maddy moaned.

"Besides, you're meeting Evie tomorrow," Mum added. Maddy huffed a little, but it was half-hearted.

"Tom?" Faye asked, looking at her husband.

"It's ok with me," he said and Molly smiled. Branden high-fived Ciara and grinned.

"Hey, can we ask Russel?" Ciara asked. "If he's ok. I think it would mean a lot to him."

"I don't see why not," Ian said.

"Maybe I should tag along," Tom said. "I mean I'm trained and we have that many kids you might need an extra hand."

"We'd appreciate it," Ruth smiled.

They fell into conversation, talking about everything from horses to shipwrecks to farms, but it was Maddy who turned the conversation to Halloween. She asked if Grandad had checked the weather that day, as he had every evening for the past week, to see if the beach party was possible.

"It still looks alright," he said.

"Great, then the wreck people can come too!" Maddy said, looking around at the team.

"What's this?" Ian asked.

"Oh, a Halloween beach party," Mum said. "It was Ciara's idea. If the weather is alright."

"That sounds fun," Jim said with a grin.

"If it isn't raining," Mum added.

"Well, if it is, why not have it at the cottage?" Ruth asked. "I mean it would be a bit spookier than here and it's close to the beach. If it starts to rain, you can make a dash for it."

"That," Grandad said. "Is a very good idea." Ruth smiled. Ciara smiled.

Halloween was looking better than ever.

Chapter 10

Russel waved at Ciara as he climbed out of the back of the car that pulled up beside Misty's stable. A woman, Ciara guessed was his mum, stepped out of the front seat clutching her purse nervously. She glanced up at Ciara with a smile.

"Hi," Ciara said while jogging over.

"Hey," Russel replied with a smile.

"You must be Ciara. I'm Russel's Mum, it's nice to meet you. None of us can thank you enough for saving Russel," the woman rushed. She hovered as if she wanted to hug Ciara but didn't know if she could. In the end, she shook Ciara's hand warmly. Russel blushed and Ciara smirked.

"It was Misty mostly," Ciara said, glancing over at the bay mare who had wandered across to the fence line to see what was going on. Russel looked over at her.

"Erm, I'd sure like to say hi to her, if that's ok," he said.

"Sure, come on."

Ciara took Russel over to meet Misty officially, while Mum came out and started chatting with Russel's mum. Misty nudged Russel gently with her soft muzzle. The boy didn't seem to know what to do around her, stiffening up as she nibbled at him. Ciara pulled a carrot out and showed him how to give it to her and after a few minutes, he seemed to relax. He was getting on pretty well with Misty when the two boys ambled over in hope of a carrot too. Russel drew back a bit as Aramis pushed his head over the fence. Ciara rubbed Aramis's neck and the grey nudged at her pocket.

"It's ok," Ciara said to Russel. "This is Aramis and Louie, they're big but they're softies really."

"They're huge," Russel said. "I thought Misty was big!" Ciara smiled. Russel's mum came over and met Misty too.

"Anna is going to stay here with me," Mum said, leaning on the fence near Misty and glancing at Russel's mum. "While you go out with Tom and the team."

"Ok," Ciara said with a smile. "We should get going really. You ready?" she asked Russel. He nodded. "Where's Branden?"

"Oh, he went down early, he'll meet you at the beach," Mum said with a smile.

Ciara and Russel walked in silence towards Molly's house, neither one sure what to say. Molly sat on the gate when they arrived. She waved and hopped down.

"The team's gone down to the cove already, I said I'd wait for you," Molly said smiling. "Hi Russel, how are you? Ok now?"

Russel just nodded and Molly dropped the subject. They walked down to the sand together chatting about the doubloon and the wreck. When they finally broke through the dunes though Russel fell silent and shuddered as he looked out over the jutting black rocks.

"You don't have to come," Ciara said. She looked out at the crashing waves, they weren't nearly as high as they had been when Ciara had pulled Russel out, but they looked equally cold.

"No," Russel said. "I want to go."

Tom jogged over the sand towards them smiling and Molly waved at him.

"Hi Dad, we're all here," she said.

"Excellent," Tom said. "Well, the team's ready. We'll do a quick safety chat and then go on in ok?"

They all nodded and followed Tom over to the outcrop. Ciara had never spent much time close up to the black rocks, and every time she did, she was amazed at how big they actually were. Standing next to the outcrop, it was well above her head height. She glanced at Russel wondering what it would have been like being washed off something so high up. She shuddered.

Ian, Ruth, and Mandy were sorting out some equipment, while Branden was helping Jim take some things from the inflatable boat, Branden looked up and waved at them as they approached. Tom waved back and Jim hopped out of the boat. He and Branden headed over to join them by the rocks, bringing a few bags and an armful of things that looked to Ciara like giant headcollars.

"Hey, welcome everyone, I'm Jim, I'm going to be in charge of today's outing ok," everyone nodded. "Good. So, we're just going to have a little chat about safety before we get going. We don't want any accidents." Ciara knew Jim didn't mean anything by the comment, it sounded like a speech he'd done several times before and had just fallen into, still, she saw Russel wince at his words a little. Jim didn't seem to notice. "As you can see there are several rings fastened to the rocks," he pointed at some metal loops that had been driven into the solid black rock, a long line of metal cord ran between them. "We're going to put on these harnesses," he held up one of the headcollar-like things, that made a lot more sense now. "You'll clip onto the cord just as a precaution, ok?" Again they all nodded. "When we reach a loop, we unclip and reclip onto the other side of the loop. Any questions?" There was silence and Jim smiled before glancing at Mandy.

"Ok then," she said. "The aim of today is twofold; we're going to use the better weather to get a few good photos of the wreck and of some of the parts and details which can identify her. We're also going to check out the cave we found yesterday. Ruth and Ian are going to do the pictures, Jim, Tom, and I will take you kids into the cave. Afterward, we'll meet up for lunch and swap details. OK?"

"Yeah!"

"Alright then," Jim grinned.

Jim helped fasten everyone into their harnesses and they headed over to the rocks. Ciara found herself climbing up the black surface. Russel struggled to get up, but both she and Molly pretended it was just like mounting one of the ponies and scrambled up quite easily. Once they were up on top of the black ledge, Mandy took the lead, followed by Molly, Russel, Branden, Ciara, and then Jim. They clipped onto the metal line and began to inch along the rock carefully. Below them, the motor of the little boat fired up and Ciara glanced over to see Ruth and Ian heading out over the water towards the smashed ship.

The black rock was slippery under Ciara's feet, but it was also hard and jagged. As they made their way along it, she realised just why Grandad didn't want them playing on it. In a way Russel had been lucky he hadn't hit the rocks when he fell. His accident could have been so much worse in so many ways. Ciara glanced at Russel, eyeing the waves as they walked. She wondered how far along he had been when he was washed over. The waves seemed low today and Ciara realised it was because it must have been close to low tide. Still, the spray from the breaking waves splashed at Ciara's shoes now that they were on the part of the outcrop that jutted into the sea itself.

Trying not to think about the sea, Ciara fixed her sights on the wreck. Being on the ledge gave her quite a good view of its hulking timbers. She imagined it had once been large and proud and it was sort of sad to see it so broken and crushed on the rock. Up ahead she realised Mandy had turned around a little bend she hadn't even realised was there. As she came closer she found that the outcrop flattened out just a little, and, hidden by several other veins of rock, was a tiny inlet.

The inlet was too small for a ship to travel up, but Ciara could imagine that a row boat might just fit through it. Mandy was following the line down into the inlet. A rock ledge ran parallel to the water, just wide enough to walk along safely. Ciara picked her way down, feeling excited and a little anxious. She almost felt like she was in an old movie searching some lost remote island for hidden treasure.

The group gathered together at a little sheltered spot just inside what was clearly a cave. The sea here lapped gently against the cavern floor. Mandy unlipped her harness and set it on a hook.

"This is as far as we've been," she said with a smile. "But from here on out we're on dry land, so the harnesses shouldn't be necessary."

They all began to unclip and Jim gathered everything up, keeping them together. He glanced at his watch. "Ok, we have about 45 minutes to explore. After that the tide will start coming in again and it'll be trickier to walk out. So, we're going into the cave for no more than twenty minutes, ok?" Everyone nodded. "Ok then."

They began to walk deeper into the cave. No one seemed to want to talk, too busy looking around the strange cave for any signs of life from the past. The floor was sandy, which surprised Ciara, she'd expected more black rock.

"This is amazing," Russel said quietly as they followed Jim.

"It is pretty cool," Branden said.

The cave narrowed and then split off into two different directions. They all gathered together at the fork glancing down in both directions. Jim flashed a light down both routes.

"Well, looks like we have a choice

to make," he said.

Mandy pulled her flashlight out too and began playing its beam of light over the walls and floor. Everyone strained to see what might be there, but all Ciara could make out was rock. She was starting to think that neither route would lead to much when Russel called out.

"Look," he had been staring into the other tunnel, shining his own little light down it. Everyone gathered around to see what he had found. "Watch!"

He flicked the beam of light down the cavern wall. Halfway down something reflected the light making it shine a little. Jim frowned, he pulled out his torch and shone it. The same thing happened, though Ciara couldn't tell why.

"Should we check it out?" he said.

"Yeah," Mandy grinned.

They began to walk down the cavern towards whatever was making the light flare. Soon enough they were at the spot, Jim shone his light over the walls and then chuckled.

"Well would you look at that," he said. He reached over and picked up the old miner's lamp lodged in a nook in the wall. "Well, at least someone has been here before."

"Wow," Russel said, staring at the lamp. "Could it have been smugglers?"

"Maybe," Jim said. "It's old

enough."

"Since there's evidence people went this way, maybe we should keep going," Mandy suggested.

They all agreed and began to walk further into the cavern, scanning the walls and floor as they went. Not much further into the cave, Branden spotted something on the floor.

"What is that?" he asked. Stooping down he picked up a coil of rope covered in dust and sand.

"Still on the right track," Jim said, clapping him on the shoulder.

"Would you look at that?" Mandy said a little further on.

The group hurried to catch up with her. Ciara came to a halt beside her and stared as Mandy played her light around the end of the cave. It was full of old dusty barrels, a few crates, lamps like the one they had found earlier and odd coils of rope.

"This could easily have been somewhere that smuggled goods were kept," Mandy said.

"You think there are still things in the crates and barrels?" Russel asked.

"Are you hoping for more doubloons?" Molly said with a smile.

Russel shrugged but smirked. "Maybe."

"Let's take a careful look," Jim said. They crowded around as he lifted the lid on a barrel, but it was empty, as was the one next to it.

"Try the crate," Mandy said.

The crate had been upturned, and when Jim righted it, they all knew instantly it was empty from the large hole in its side. A murmur of disappointment flitted around.

"Hey now," Jim said. "Let's not get too down, we've found some history here. You know finding this lamp is as important as finding gold."

"But maybe not as exciting," Branden whispered.

"Hold up," Mandy said. She dusted something off that had been laying by the crate and picked it up. It was a little candle stick holder, the chunky base a little dinted on one side. "You know what this is?"

"A candlestick?" Tom suggested.

Jim took it off Mandy with a smile. "This isn't just any old candlestick," he beamed in the light of the torch. "Well, well."

"What is it?" Ciara asked.

"This," Mandy said, pointing at the little object. "Is good evidence Russel's story has some truth to it."

Russel frowned. "That isn't treasure though," he said.

"It sort of is," Jim replied. "It's Spanish, and from the 1500s. It's made of brass. They called them reels, because of the base shape, see?

He held up the little candlestick so they could see its shape. It was hard in the darkness of the cave, but

Ciara could just make out the bottom of it, Jim was right, it looked just like a reel you'd find thread or rope on.

"So, this came from the wreck?" Branden said.

"We can't prove it entirely, but it seems likely," Jim said. "Probably Russel's story is true, perhaps the smugglers didn't find a ton of loot. The Armada was made up of treasure ships, but they could certainly have stripped out silverware, things like this, other pieces."

"Wow," Ciara said. She looked over at Russel who was staring at the little brass candle holder. She wasn't sure in the dim light, but she thought there may be tears running silently down his face. He'd done what he wanted to do, prove that his Grandad's story was true, or at any rate likely to be.

"What happens to the candlestick now?" Ciara asked.

"We'll log it with any other finds from the wreck and it'll go to the local archive," Mandy replied.

"Does it have to?" Ciara asked, a thought popping into her mind. "I mean, if there was a museum locally that could take it and put it on display, would that be ok?"

"Yeah," Jim said. "I should think so."

"What are you thinking?" Molly asked.

"That we should ask Orla and her Dad if it could go to the castle. They're putting a display together anyway, wouldn't it be cool to have something on the wreck in it?" Ciara said.

"Yeah," Molly smiled. "They could put something up about Russel's Grandad's story!"

Russel looked up at Ciara and Molly wide-eyed and Ciara grinned. "Can we ask before you send it to the archive?" she said to Mandy. "Orla's not back until after Halloween."

"That's ok," Jim said with a shrug. "You ask, I'll drag my feet over the paperwork until you have."

"Yes," Mandy chuckled. "Because

you never do that anyway."

"Hey!" Jim exclaimed and everyone giggled.

"Hate to break up the party," Tom said. "But we're 25 minutes in, time to turn back."

Mandy put the little candlestick into a finds bag and placed it in her backpack before they began to head back. As they headed out of the cave, Ciara stumbled. Branden caught her.

"You ok?" he asked.

"Yeah, my foot caught on something," she reached down and tugged at whatever her foot had snagged.

The piece of metal she freed was familiar enough to her. Twisted a little, and missing some parts, Ciara knew it was curb bit instantly, she held it up for Mandy. She smiled broadly at Ciara.

"And several white horses swam ashore," she said, shaking her head as she pulled out another finds bag. "I guess they swam there, not wearing any tack."

"Is that from the ship too?" Molly asked. Mandy nodded with a grin.

"Trust you to find something horsey in a cave," Branden smiled, nudging Ciara. "Come on, before we all get stuck in here."

Ciara smiled and followed her brother back out towards the craggy rocks and the wrecked ship, her thoughts drifting to the horses that survived the wreck.

Chapter 11

Ciara sat staring out of her bedroom window at the moonlit yard below. The silvery light cast long shadows by the stables. Aramis put his head over the door, the pale light making him look even whiter than usual, like a ghost horse, Ciara thought with a smile. She'd struggled to sleep that night, her mind a whir of thoughts, maybe it was the excitement of the day, but she couldn't stop thinking about the horse bit she'd stumbled over.

When she had first held it in her

hand, she'd simply recognised what it was, an old curb-style bit. Once they were back on the beach though her mind began to wander to who it had belonged to. Not the human so much, from what she'd learnt there were no survivors from the shipwreck. The horses though, some of them had swum ashore if the local legend was to be believed. Had the bit belonged to one of them? Ciara decided she hoped it did, the thought of the horses in the sea made her heartache.

She remembered how scared she'd been on Misty, striding out through the cold water towards Russel. They had been on the sandy shelf, and the sea had been relatively calm. There'd been a storm the night of the shipwreck. Ciara had seen the cove when a storm hit. The waves would lash the beach, grow fearsome and frothy. The sound of the crashing water alone was deafening without the addition of rain or lightning. The idea of a horse being out in it made her blood run cold as Grandad would say.

Ciara stared out towards the cove picturing the ship in her mind, being tossed about in the sea and breaking up. Men and horses leaping into the water to try any way they could to escape to safety. Her heart pounded as she imagined a grey horse, the one she pictured in her mind when she thought of the bit. He would have been frightened, surrounded by sea and a broken ship. He'd swim, not sure where to go, panicked. Maybe his foot hit the sand bar and he scrabbled for it, a bit of security. There were other horses too, perhaps they followed him to the sand bar, standing on it just where Misty had when they pulled in Russel.

The horses would follow the land, feeling the solid ground under their feet, then they'd see the shore, safety, and rush for it. They'd serge out of the water like one of the white-crested waves and jump onto the sand shaking and wild-eyed, longing to run away from the sea and the cold but not sure where to dart. Ciara wondered who first found them on the sands. In her daydream she pictured herself there with Misty, going up to the long-maned grey horse and telling him it was alright, that he and his friends were safe, they just had to follow Misty. Ciara yawned.

She slipped down under the covers. She shivered just a little, it was turning colder. In the summer cool sheets were a welcome thing, now though she felt glad when the bed started to warm up around her. She snuggled deeper, still thinking about the ship and the horses. Tomorrow was Halloween, the night of the lantern ride and the party. It was fitting really, Ciara mused, to find the wreck and the bit so close to a holiday about ghosts and spooky things. As she closed her eyes there was the distant sound of thunder and the wind picked up just a little, whistling around the house. Maddy stirred in her bed, and Kit woke up for a second, pressing himself closer to her before putting his nose on his paws and closing his eyes again. Ciara smiled and let her own eyes drop shut, still picturing swimming horses and broken ships.

The storm that raged through the night left everything wet, but the sun dawned bright and the sky clear. Ciara shuffled into breakfast feeling a little groggy after her late night but cheered up when she saw Mum had made ghost-shaped pancakes for breakfast.

"Look, chocolate eyes!" Maddy said with a grin as she drew a smiley face on her pancake with syrup. Ciara smiled.

"How's the weather looking for tonight?" she asked, sitting down. Mum handed her a pancake.

Grandad took a sip of his coffee and lowered his newspaper. "Good or bad news?" he said.

"Bad" Ciara said with a wince.

"Due rain about 8 pm," Grandad said. "Good news, alright until then, so your lantern ride to the cove is on, but I think we'll have to do the party at the cottage. Still, I have a plan."

"What plan?" Mum asked suspiciously.

Grandad chuckled. "Well, I was over at Davies yesterday and we got talking about the cottages. He reminded me we'd had a cookout there before, not long after we bought the place. We used this little old marquee tent of his to cook in and sat on some hay bales in the little barn. I thought we'd do the same. I still have the half-barrel BBQ we used, it's in the garage."

"Our hay is in big round bales though," Ciara pointed out, thinking of the huge bale they kept beside the sheep pen in a little lean-to shed.

Grandad chuckled. "Aye, but Davie

has some left over from the sheep, no good to anyone, so I'm going to fetch them today along with the little marquee. I'll set it up with Branden and we can take the old BBQ and fire pit down. Put the fire pit in the barn and the BBQ in the tent. All good for ghost stories."

"And maybe some music," Branden added, coming into the kitchen with his guitar. "Lucas is coming over and Jim said he plays a bit. I thought we'd play a few songs."

"Ah, now we have a party!" Grandad said.

Mum put some pancakes down for Branden. "How is Davie, he moves in today doesn't he?"

Grandad's face fell a little. He nodded. "Mel and I are going over this morning for a coffee before he goes."

"Did he decide what he's doing with the farm and the cottages?" Ciara asked almost without thinking.

Grandad sighed. He nodded his head. "Farm is being let out. Young girl, just finished college actually, she's local, does a lot on the eventing circuit. She's good too, professional good, she wants somewhere not too far from her folks to do up as her training facility. I think Mrs. Fitz knows her, or her younger sister," Grandad mused.

"What about Holly and Yew tree?" Mum asked, sitting down.

Grandad looked uncomfortable.

"Not sure yet," he murmured, but Ciara was pretty sure he knew and was trying to avoid talking about it. Her heart sank. That probably meant he was going to sell up. Ciara thought about Molly and Ranger, she couldn't tell them anything, because she knew nothing, she was only guessing from Grandad's behaviour.

Mum glanced from Grandad to Ciara and back. "We should get sorted for the day really, look at the time," she smiled trying to change the subject. "Lot's to do. Branden you'll help Grandad with the setup at Yew Tree won't you?" Branden nodded. "And Maddy, you give Kit a walk then help me pack up all the food. Ciara can do the same when she's finished the horses." Ciara nodded, feeling a little less enthusiastic about the day.

    The morning dragged even though Ciara had all three of the horses to turn and muck out. She couldn't help but think about Davie selling up with each fork full. She sighed as she straightened Misty's bed up. Ciara glanced over at Misty, the little mare was bossing Louie around and telling him to move. Ciara smiled. The paddock was drying out slowly, but Ciara had still put rugs on all of them, mostly to keep Misty mud free for later on. Despite everything she was looking forward to the lantern ride to the cove, she just wished she knew what to say to Molly.

It was late in the afternoon when Ciara, dressed in her pirate costume, clambered up the mounting block and slipped onto Misty's back. She had a little head torch on her helmet to light her way home, even though it would be more dusk than dark. Branden stepped up beside her carrying a lantern and holding Maddy's hand. Kit bounced at him, making little excited whimpery noises.

"Everyone ready?" he asked. Maddy nodded and giggled. "Ok, off to Molly's house we go."

"Hold on," Grandad called. He came over carrying his own lantern followed by Mum. "We're all going."

They set off walking down the driveway, Misty leading the way. The October sun was sinking into a yellow haze as they reached the dunes. From the direction of Holly and Yew Tree, a stream of torches began to wind down to meet them. Molly was there with Ranger, her parents, the whole wreck team, and Russel, as well as Niblet the donkey. Ciara knew Niblet could be ridden, but she'd never seen him in tack before, so she was surprised to see him kitted out in a bridle and little saddle pad.

"Who's riding Niblet?" she asked, glancing at Russel. He held up his hands and shook his head quickly.

Molly giggled. "I thought Maddy

might like a lift, just to the beach and back. It seemed like we should have more riders."

"Can I!" Maddy beamed. "Please!"

Grandad went to pick her up and she handed Kit's lead to Branden. "Up you go," he said, hoisting her onto Niblet. If the donkey was bothered at all he didn't show it. Tom was standing beside him, his hand on Niblet's red lead rope. Grandad stood beside Maddy, his hand steadying her just in case.

"Well," Mandy said. "I wish I had Dixie here now."

"It's quite a thing isn't it," Jim added. "A torchlight Halloween ride down to the wreck," he chuckled.

"Oddest investigation I've been on in a while."

They all began to weave their way down to the sand, chatting and laughing. Ciara sat on Misty feeling her movement as they made their way steadily through the dunes. Somehow it was peaceful and noisy all at the same time.

They broke out onto the cove and stopped. The wreck was silhouetted in black against the dusky sky, the clouds that drifted across the setting sun looked almost black, while the sea seemed to shine like a gem in the fading night.

"Now isn't that a sight," Grandad said.

Everyone nodded, but no one said a thing, they all just stood there in the fading light, the magical feeling of Halloween all around them, watching the stunning view. Ciara and Molly rode off a little way along the sand, while the walkers and Niblet crossed towards the black rocks to get a better look at the wreck. It had slipped a little during the storm the night before and the team was pretty sure she'd be lost beneath the waves again by spring. Still, it was now official, she was Spanish and very much likely to have been part of the Armada.

Ciara looked over her shoulder at the wreck as she rode along beside

Molly. "It's sort of hauntingly beautiful, isn't it?"

Molly nodded. "I think this was a great idea. It feels like, I don't know, like we're saying goodbye to the ship, giving it a Halloween send-off or something."

"It sort of does, doesn't it," Ciara said with a sad smile. She took a deep breath trying to decide if she should tell Molly her suspicions about Holly Tree. They turned to head back. "Davie moved today," Ciara began.

"I know," Molly said, not looking over at her.

"He's let the farm," Ciara said. That did make Molly look.

"And the cottages?" She asked.

Ciara shrugged. "Grandad said he didn't know but,"

"But what?" she asked.

"I don't know," Ciara said, trying to find the right words. "It was like he did know, but he didn't want to say. Or maybe he doesn't know and I'm just overthinking it. I'm not making any sense am I?"

"You sort of are," Molly said. "I get it, I'm worried too. I don't want to be, but I can't help it. I like it now you're here, we have someone to ride with and Ranger's at home. If we move it would be awful."

Ciara nodded. "I know." Glancing at the pinpricks of torch lights making their way back over the beach.

"Well, we don't know anything yet," Molly pointed out. "Besides, even if he does sell it, perhaps it'll be with us still as tenants. That happens sometimes, I've seen it on TV."

Ciara nodded. That was true. There's always hope, they had to be optimistic, that was what Olivia always told her, be optimistic, if you are good things happen. Ciara glanced at the wreck, she wondered if its crew had felt optimistic. She shuddered.

The group all joined back together and headed for home through the approaching darkness. Mum had agreed to walk back with Ciara and then drive her down to Yew Tree cottage in the car, along with Lucas who was meeting them there. As they parted ways at the gate, Ciara couldn't help but hope this wouldn't be the last Halloween ride they did together at the cove.

Chapter 12

Smoke billowed out of the side of the little marquee tent, spiralling into the black velvet night. The smell of BBQ followed it, hitting Ciara's nose as she walked towards Yew Tree cottage following her Mum. Grandad and Branden had set the marquee up right next to the little old barn, so one of its open sides was closed in by the stone wall giving the little tent some shelter. Grandad was stood in it, by one of the open sides, turning a sausage on the BBQ fashioned out of half of an old metal barrel.

Molly waved Ciara over to the barn and she jogged across. The wreck team had emptied the barn out, putting their equipment away in their vehicles ready to leave in the morning. In its place were several hay bales. Ruth, Ian, and Mandy were sat on a couple, laughing and drinking something out of paper cups. Branden, Lucas, and Jim were fiddling with guitars, huddled together by the back wall chatting about music as they tightened strings and tuned up. Ciara realised it would be strange to see the team go in a way.

Ciara sat beside Molly, Russel, and Maddy, who was playing with Kit and trying to keep him away from the smell of the BBQ. Ciara scratched at his ears and he licked her hand hopefully.

"It smells great," Molly said. "I'm so hungry."

"Umm," Ciara nodded. "It does smell nice." She wanted to say something more about the cottages, but she wasn't sure what. She was about to say something when Jim piped up from the back of the barn.

"So, music first or stories?" he asked with a smile.

"Music!" The wreck team all cheered, lifting their cups. Ciara and Molly laughed and nodded.

"Why don't you all go in the kitchen and grab a drink," Mum said, coming in with a paper cup. "Before they start."

Ciara nodded and jumped up; she headed inside the cottage through the open door. It was the first time she'd been inside since Branden and Lucas had painted some of it. She paused and looked in at the living room. The walls had been decorated in a light, sandy yellow colour, it made the dark wooden beam above the stove really stand out. Ciara liked it. The 'rugs' hid most of the bare floorboards too and it looked much better, more homely.

"It looks nice, doesn't it?" Ciara turned to see Grandad stood behind her. She smiled and nodded.

"It looks cleaner and a lot warmer. It just needs a carpet, and the bathroom doing," Ciara said wrinkling her nose as she thought about the old bathroom with its mismatched walls and toilet.

Grandad chuckled. "That it does, but it'll get there."

"Does that mean you're going to finish fixing it up?" Ciara asked.

Grandad nodded. "I had a chat with Branden and Lucas about it earlier. They're going to help me do it. Well, most of it, I think we'll get an actual plumber in to do the bathroom. I don't fancy tackling pipework. The rest I can do though, show them how to tile and such like.

You and Maddy might want to help too, might come in useful when you're bigger."

Ciara smiled. "I like painting," she said. Grandad gave her a hug. "What will you do when it's all finished though? I mean it's sort of partly yours, right? You and Davie bought it together."

Grandad nodded again. "It is. I'm not 100% certain what I'll do yet. I have a couple of thoughts, chatted over things a bit with Davie, but, well, we'll see. Come on, let's get you that drink, it sounds like they're starting up."

Grandad guided her towards the kitchen. Ciara poured herself a cup of juice and headed back into the night wondering what Grandad might do with the cottage. It was smaller than Holly Tree, but maybe it could be extended so Molly could stay there if Davie sold up. Ciara shook the thought from her head, it just wasn't big enough to do that, nor was there really any room for Niblet and Ranger. Ciara sighed. The first stings of music drifted out into the darkness as Ciara wandered over to the little barn. Jim, Lucas, and Branden started up a song and Ciara sat down on the closest bale listening as she sipped at her juice.

They played several songs, some Halloween based, some sea shanties that Jim knew, which seemed perfect given the wreck's proximity. The rest of the wreck team even joined in singing some of them, even Grandad seemed to know a few, Ciara could hear him singing along from the marquee as he tended the BBQ. They'd just finished a really upbeat tune when Grandad stuck his head in through the open door with a smile.

"Food's ready, come grab it while it's hot," he said.

Everyone shuffled out and into the marquee, grabbing potatoes, sausages, and other goodies Grandad had cooked for them. Ciara paused as she stepped out into the night, looking out over the cliffs in the direction she knew the wreck would be. With the

Halloween darkness all around her, she took a moment to just think about the ship and the horses. The memories of last night came into her mind, the daydream of seeing the horses swimming to the shore. Russel stepped up beside her.

"It's odd, isn't it? Knowing there's a shipwreck so close to us on Halloween," he said. Ciara smiled and nodded.

It had started to drizzle a little, turning cooler, Ciara turned and headed into the little marquee to grab something to eat. Russel followed her with another glance over his shoulder in the direction of the wreck. The heat from the BBQ was welcome, and

Ciara liked the feel of it washing over her as she helped herself to a baked potato, a couple of sausages, and a corn on the cob. She carried her plate back to the barn, trying to dodge the rain as she went. Inside the barn, it was a little chilly, even with everyone huddled in it. For a second, she thought about suggesting moving into the cottage itself, but that wouldn't be the same. There was something about sitting in the barn, with its rough walls and bare floor. It fitted with Halloween more than the cottage, especially since it had been decorated a bit more. Mum and Faye handed out several blankets and Grandad lit a little stove in the barn, its chimney poked out through a little hole in the barn wall.

They settled down eating and chatting, and soon enough it was much warmer, even as the rain began to fall more steadily outside. Maddy slipped some sausage down to Kit and Ciara smirked. The conversation slowly turned to the wreck.

"Did you find anything else when we left?" Russel asked, around a mouthful of sausage sandwich.

"We did!" Ruth said excitedly. "We sent our little ROV down and saw some great stuff."

"What's a ROV?" Maddy asked, slipping more sausage to Kit.

"Remotely operated vehicle," Ian

said. "Like a remote-control car, only this one goes in the water, it can take pictures and videos of things under the sea in places or conditions we wouldn't or couldn't dive in."

"And it pictured a cannon," Ruth said with a smile. "It's a perfect fit for a Spanish Armada ship, it's just the extra proof we needed."

"Wow," Russel said. "I wish I could see it."

"Maybe you will," Ian smiled. "We're planning to come back in the spring and dive the wreck, maybe bring a few finds up too. The weather should be better for it then and we can use Betsie."

"Betsie?" Molly asked.

"Ruth's camper van," Mandy giggled.

"I am not staying in a tent," Jim said, shaking his head. "No way, I hate the tent."

"You can stay in the horse box with me," Mandy smiled.

"It'll probably be more comfortable than Betsie," Ian said under his breath.

"Hey," Ruth said, shoving his shoulder. Jim laughed.

"Should we tell ghost stories now?" Maddy asked.

"Just a second," Tom said. He stood in the doorway with his arm around Faye. "We have a bit of news." Everyone turned to look at him, Molly grabbed Ciara's hand and she squeezed it.

"Most of you here know Davie Hallett, and that he moved in with his daughter, Megan today," Faye said. "And I know a lot of you, Molly and Ciara especially, were wondering what Davie was going to do with Holly Tree cottage."

Tom took over, he looked serious. "When Davie bought the cottage originally, it was to make sure it wasn't developed. He wanted the cove to stay as it was, and, well, so do we. So, Faye and I approached Davie a couple of days ago, and long story short, we offered to buy Holly Tree cottage." A wide smile spread across his face.

Molly stood up, her mouth hanging

open, one hand still clutching Ciara's. "Wait, what?"

Tom laughed. "We signed the papers this morning," he said. "Holly Tree is ours."

Molly rushed over to hug her parents, so happy she started to cry a little. Ciara looked over at Grandad, stood smirking by the doorway. She stood up and sneaked over to stand by him.

"You knew, didn't you?" she said.

Grandad smiled. "Might have done, but if I did I couldn't exactly say anything and ruin a good surprise now could I?" Ciara shook her head and then grinned. Grandad pulled her into a hug.

"Well now, this really is a celebration," Jim said. "Hold on a second, I have something. I was saving it until later, but now seems like a good time."

He disappeared inside the cottage for a few moments and came back carrying two glass bottles. "Champers for the grown-ups and sparkling elderflower for the young ones," he said with a smile. "Nipped down the shops earlier. It was meant to be a thank you for letting us use the cottage, but I think this is a better reason to pop them open, don't you think?"

There were cheers all around and a popping sound as the corks pinged out of the two bottles. Jim poured everyone a glass and they sat down happily.

"Can we please tell spooky stories now?" Maddy asked plaintively. Everyone chuckled.

"Ok, ok, I'll start," Branden said. "I have a great one."

They settled down together, gathered in the warm light of the stove listening to Branden's story. Ciara had heard it before, she found her mind wandering from his tale to the wreck, to the fact Molly was definitely staying. She smiled; her world felt somehow a little more secure.

It was late when they got back

home. Maddy had fallen asleep and Branden had to carry her upstairs to bed, Kit padding along at his heels, his tail drooping from sheer fatigue. As Ciara followed him upstairs she heard Mum's phone ring. She shrugged, too tired to think who would be calling this late at night.

Branden placed Maddy in bed and she stirred a little. Mum had said it was ok for her to sleep in her costume, just for once, it was made up of soft materials anyway. Branden drew the blanket over her and Kit hopped up on the bed, snuggling into her. He smiled.

"Night," he whispered to Ciara.

"Night," she said back.

Branden headed to his own room and closed the door behind him. Ciara went to start pulling her costume off but stopped. She forgot she'd left her clean pyjama bottoms downstairs. With a sigh, she crept out of her room and started downstairs. Grandad was nowhere to be seen, but Mum was in the kitchen talking to someone on speakerphone. She was smiling broadly. Ciara crept closer, realising the voice on the phone was Dad's. He never called late, he always wanted to speak to them too. Ciara felt her heart race hoping nothing was wrong.

"When?" Mum said.

"I finish up December 9th," Dad's voice said. "I'll be back in time for the Christmas plays, the works."

"That's amazing," Mum said. "The kids will be so excited!"

Ciara felt a smile spread over her face. Dad was coming home! Her smile froze, Dad was coming home. What would that mean, what about Misty, Kit, Grandad? She swallowed hard.

"You sure Pat will be ok with us all crashing his house until we find a place?" Dad said. "I mean, I can start looking, so could you."

"Dad'll be fine, we can look together when you're back," Mum said.

Ciara crept out of the front door. She could feel the sting of tears on her cheeks as she dashed across the black darkness of the yard and into Misty's stable. She flung her arms around the bay mare's neck, burying her face in her soft, warm coat. She felt more torn than she could ever remember. Ciara had hated it when Dad left to work away, all she had wanted was for him to stay. Even knowing she wanted him back so badly it hurt and she was happy he was coming home. At the same time though her world had changed. She loved having Misty at home, to ride every day. There was Grandad, she'd learnt so much from him and he clearly liked having them around. If they went back to the city he'd be alone. Ciara swallowed a sob that tried to escape her. She didn't want to leave Coral Cove. She liked her school, Molly, heck she'd even grown a bit more friendly with Russel.

Ciara couldn't imagine leaving now. Not getting to ride on the beach at sunset with Misty, unless they were visiting on holiday. Then there was Maddy. Ciara thought about her snuggled up with Kit. He was Grandad's dog really, would Dad even agree to let him come live with them? If he didn't there would be one miserable dog and an even more miserable Maddy. It was so unfair. Why couldn't Dad come home and they all live together?

The clouds cleared a little and

the moonlight shone into Misty's stable. The cool October breeze ruffled Ciara's costume and she snuggled closer to Misty, the mare seemed to pull her closer.

"Why does everything change when I don't want it to," she said in a low voice. Misty said nothing, but she did rub a little at Ciara's arm as if to say it would be alright. Just a few hours ago Ciara had been worried it was Molly who would move away, now it looked like it would be her. She stood holding tightly to Misty. Would she be able to take Misty with her wherever they went? Dad might agree to find a stable close to them they could rent. Then again, there was always the possibility that like Kit, Misty would remain at Grandad's and she would go without her. Ciara glanced at the Halloween night.

"Please let it be ok," she said, staring at the bright round moon. "Please."

Enjoy the next book in the series:

THE CORAL COVE SERIES

www.writtenbyelaine.com

www.ingramcontent.com/pod-product-compliance
Lightning Source LLC
Chambersburg PA
CBHW030033100526
44590CB00011B/187